Books by Brander Matthews

These Many Years, Recollections of a New Yorker

BIOGRAPHIES

Shakspere as a Playwright
Molière, His Life and His Works

ESSAYS AND CRITICISMS

The Principles of Playmaking
French Dramatists of the 19th Century
Pen and Ink, Essays on subjects of more or less
    importance
Aspects of Fiction, and other Essays
The Historical Novel, and other Essays
Parts of Speech, Essays on English
The Development of the Drama
Inquiries and Opinions
The American of the Future, and other Essays
Gateways to Literature, and other Essays
On Acting
A Book About the Theater
Essays on English

Vignettes of Manhattan; Outlines in Local Color

THE PRINCIPLES OF
PLAYMAKING

THE PRINCIPLES OF PLAYMAKING

AND OTHER DISCUSSIONS OF THE DRAMA

BY

BRANDER MATTHEWS

PROFESSOR OF DRAMATIC LITERATURE IN COLUMBIA UNIVERSITY
MEMBER OF THE AMERICAN ACADEMY OF ARTS AND LETTERS

NEW YORK
CHARLES SCRIBNER'S SONS
1922

TO
GUSTAVE LANSON

CONTENTS

vii

THE PRINCIPLES OF PLAYMAKING

I

OF all the theorists of the theater in the nine-teenth century Francisque Sarcey was the shrewdest. He had an incomparable intimacy with the drama and an insatiable desire to dis-cover the principles of the art of playmaking. Yet when he once set out to discuss these prin-ciples he felt obliged to begin by disclaiming any intention of issuing a series of edicts to be obeyed to the letter by all intending playwrights. "Most readers," he declared, "when you speak to them of a treatise on the art of the theater, or to ex-press it more simply, as did our fathers, when you speak to them of the Rules of the Drama, believe that you have in mind a code of precepts by the aid of which one is assured, if he writes, of com-posing a piece without faults, or if he criticizes, of being able to place his finger precisely on every defect." Sarcey went on to confess that this be-lief in the all-sufficiency of a sequence of dramatic dogmas was peculiarly French and that it was a long establisht tradition. He cited the case of the worthy Abbé d'Aubignac in the seventeenth century, who promulgated a code for dramatic literature (translated into English under the significant title of the 'Whole Art of the Stage'), and who was tempted later to compose a tragedy "according to his own formula and made it prodigiously tiresome,"—a misadventure which has "never cured the public of its belief in the efficacy of Rules."

Then Sarcey declared that he did not purpose to formulate any Rules, to promulgate any Laws, to mint any Maxims or to present any Precepts; what he proposed to himself was to seek out the underlying Principles of playmaking by a disinterested attempt to ascertain the actual basis of the drama and by seizing upon the essential conditions of this art, which differentiate it from all the other arts. And he found this actual basis in the fact that "the word *play* carries with it the idea of an audience. We cannot conceive of a play without an audience." All the accessories of performance, scenery and costumes, the stage itself and its footlights, these the drama can get along without, but the audience is indispensable. "A dramatic work, whatever it may be, is designed to be witnest by a number of persons united and forming an audience; that is its very essence; that is one indispensable condition of its existence. The audience is the necessary and inevitable condition to which dramatic art must

2

accommodate its means." As it is almost impossible to gather exactly the same audience two or three times in succession, and as no audience can be kept interested for more than a few hours at a sitting, it is a principle of playmaking that the dramatist must devise a dominating action and that he must condense his story, dealing only with its most interesting moments and presenting it shorn of all negligible details. And as an audience is a crowd, composed of all sorts and conditions of men, the dramatist must deal with subjects appealing to collective human nature and he must eschew themes of a more limited attraction.

Other critics before Sarcey had suggested that the playwright had always to pay attention to the desires and to the demands of the playgoers. In the sixteenth century Castelvetro had had more than a glimpse of this truth. In the seventeenth century Molière had boldly declared that the one duty of the dramatist was to please the public; and Corneille had said the same thing but characteristically with more caution. In the eighteenth century, Marmontel, a playwright himself as well as a theorist of the theater, had asserted that the first duty of the dramatist was "to move the spectators, and the second is to move them only in so far as they are willing to be moved," which will depend "on the disposition and the manners of the people to whom appeal is

made, and on the degree of sensibility they bring
to the theater." And in the nineteenth century,
—and after Sarcey had started his inquiry—
Brunetière insisted that "a play does not begin
to exist as a play except before the footlights, by
virtue of the collaboration and of the complicity
of the public, without which a play never has been
and never can be anything more than a mere
literary exercise."

Sarcey had made his declaration of faith in
1876; and ten years later, Bronson Howard,
wholly unfamiliar with the French critic's articles,
expounded a doctrine almost identical, in the lec-
ture which he entitled the 'Autobiography of a
Play.' He called attention to the fact that
Æschylus, Sophocles and Euripides "did not
create the laws of dramatic construction" since
"those laws exist in the passions and sympathies
of the human race. They existed thousands of
years before the Father of the Drama was born,—
waiting, like the other laws of nature to be discovered and utilized by man." The American
playwright declared that the dramatist could
succeed only by obeying these laws, altho "no
man knows much about them. . . . When all
the mysteries of humanity have been solved, the
laws of dramatic construction can be codified
and clearly explained; not until then." It is
true that "a few general principles have been discovered by experiment and discussion"; and

yet every playwright is under the imperative necessity of obeying all the principles of the art, even those he has not discovered. Fortunately, "the art of obeying them is merely the art of using your common sense in the study of your own and other people's emotions."

II

In the epitaph written by Pope we are told that

Nature and Nature's laws lay hid in night:
God said, "Let Newton be!" and all was light.

But Newton's Law is only one of Nature's laws; it declares only one of the principles which control the visible universe; and no Newton has yet arisen to declare the principles which control dramatic construction. These principles however have been obeyed unwittingly by all the great dramatists, ancient and modern. The Rules laid down tentatively or arbitrarily by the theorists of theater are but groping efforts to grasp the undying principles which we can seize only unsatisfactorily, which "exist in the passions and sympathies of the human race," and which are never completely disclosed to anyone, not even if he is possest of the piercing insight of Aristotle. No doubt, this is just as true of painting and of sculpture as it is of the drama. The principles of the pictorial art and of the plastic art have been de-

clared with certainty and with finality by no
critic, not even by Lessing.

The principle of Nature which causes an apple
to fall from a tree is eternal; it existed and did
its work long before Newton was able to formulate
the Law of Gravitation; and it would continue
to exist and to do its work even if some later and
greater Newton should some day be able to prove
that Newton's Law is not just what he asserted
it to be. What is true of Newton's Law in
mechanics is true also of Gresham's Law in finance
and of Grimm's Law in philology. It is no less
true of Brunetière's Law in the drama. The stalwart French critic contended that what differen-
tiates the drama from the epic is the necessity the
play is under of presenting strong-willed creatures
engaged in a tense struggle of clashing volitions;
and the principles of dramatic construction, whatever they may be, remain just what they were,
and what they had always been before Brunetière
made his suggestive and instructive effort to reduce one of these principles to a formally stated
Law. In other words, Newton's Law and Gresham's and Grimm's and Brunetière's are not
strictly speaking "laws" at all; they are only
working hypotheses, which seem to square with
the fact so far as we have been able to ascertain it.

The Rules of the Drama which were formulated
in the classicist code by the supersubtle Italian
critics of the Renascence, Castelvetro, Mintorno

6

and the rest, were accepted by the profest critics of all the other nations, altho the professional playwrights of England and of Spain refused to be driven into the triple-barred cage of the Unities and declined to deprive themselves of the privilege of commingling the comic with the tragic or to force themselves to fill out the artificial framework of five acts. Lessing battered a breach in the classicist citadel; and it was finally stormed and sacked by the fiery French romanticists of 1830. The Rules of the classicists were elaborated by pedants, who had no intimate acquaintance with the actual theater, where alone the principles of dramatic construction can be seen at work. It is more than probable that Castelvetro and Mintorno had neither of them ever seen a good play well acted before any other audience than an invited assembly of dilettants; and it is no wonder that their Rules were found to lack validity when put to the test in the theater itself.

Far more valuable are the rough-and-ready Maxims, the bread-and-butter Precepts, which the old stager is forever impressing upon the young playwright. These Precepts and these Maxims, handed down from generation to generation, studio-traditions so to speak, are valid, as far as they go. They are efforts to codify the practice of contemporary playwrights and to put into useful words the common sense of these playwrights and their study of their own emotions and of the emotions of their fellows. They may not be adequate expressions of the eternal principles of playmaking, which exist and have always existed "in the passions and sympathies of the human race"; but they stand on a solider foundation, whatever their imcompleteness, than any of the alleged Rules of the pedantic theorists, ignorant of the actual theater with its actual audience.

"Never keep a secret from the audience"!—"Never try to fool the audience!"—"Begin in the thick of the action, and quit when you are thru!"—"Show every thing that is important to the plot; don't tell about it merely, but let the spectators see it for themselves!"—these are all monitions of indisputable importance; and the 'prentice playwright will do well to get them by heart and to take them to heart. He will even find profit in recalling the advice of the wily old stage-manager to J. R. Planché: "If you want to make the British public understand what you are doing, you must tell them that you are *going* to do it,—later you must tell them that you *are* doing it—finally you must tell them that you *have* done it; and then—confound them! perhaps they will understand you!" This cynical and contemptuous saying reveals itself as only a brutal over-statement of the undying principle that the audience needs ever to know what has happened so that it may have its interest aroused in what is about to happen. This is the principle which imposes upon the dramatist the duty of always being so clear that he cannot be misunderstood even by the most inattentive spectator.

The difficulty of perceiving the eternal principles of the dramatic art, and the distinction between these eternal principles and the rule-of-thumb precepts, will be found clearly exprest in Weil's 'Etudes sur le Drame Antique,' from which this suggestive passage may be borrowed: "Poetry has its laws, natural, necessary, inherent in the nature of things; it has also its traditional rules, variable, due to habit, consecrated by inheritance. The natural laws scarcely need to be declared as they can be understood without effort; but easy to seize they are none the less difficult to declare. Genius follows them instinctively; ordinary talent may hear them set forth without being able to conform to them. The traditional rules may also have a foundation; but they are for a time only, and they may become a restraint for the artist, a curb rather than a salutary check; they cannot be devined, but must be formulated to have the force of law."

III

No one of these rule-of-thumb admonitions is older than that which advises the dramatist to show everything that is important and to make it take place before the eyes of the spectators. We can find it set forth in the shrewd epistle of good counsel that Horace wrote to the son of an old friend when that youth began to manifest literary ambitions:—

> The events, which plays are written to unfold,
> Are either shown upon the stage, or told.
> Most true, whate'er's transmitted thru the ear
> To mind and heart will never come so near,
> As what is set before the eyes, and each
> Spectator sees, brought full within his reach.
> Yet do not drag upon the stage what might
> Be much more fitly acted out of sight;
> Much, too, there is which 'twill be always well
> To leave the actor's well-graced speech to tell.
> Let not Medea kill her boys in view,—
>
> .   .   .   .
>
> If things like these before my eyes be thrust,
> I turn away in sceptical disgust.

There was no living Latin drama when Horace made these suggestions; and he was proclaiming the practice of the Greek dramatic poets, when he warned the youthful playmaker not to let Medea destroy her children in view of the spectators. The actors of the Attic drama were raised aloft on thick-soled boots and they wore towering masks, and therefore they could not indulge in any violent gestures; they could neither kill nor be killed without danger of tripping and of thereby disarranging the mask, a misadventure which would be unseemly. Yet this reservation, scarcely more than suggested by Horace, was by the Italian theorists tightened into a rigorous restriction of action. In England, for example, the first five-act tragedy in blank verse is 'Gorbuduc,' in which little or nothing happens before the eyes of the spectators, altho the story itself is filled with violent horrors, all of which are decorously and dully narrated by subsidiary characters. And in France the classicists came in time almost to eschew visible action and to abound in rhetorical description of things not seen.

In Victor Hugo's famous preface to his unacted and unactable 'Cromwell,' an essay which may be accepted as the Declaration of Independence of the romanticists, he protested against the deadening results of obedience to this law by the feebler followers of Voltaire and Racine. "Instead of actions we have narratives, instead of pictures we have descriptions. Solemn personages placed, like the ancient chorus between us and the drama, come to tell us what is being done in the temple, in the palace, in the public square, until we are often tempted to cry out to them, 'Really,—then take us there! It seems to be amusing; it ought to be interesting to see!' To which they would no doubt reply, 'It is possible

11

that it would amuse and interest you, but that is not the question: we are the guardians of the dignity of Melpomene in France!' And there you are!"

Yet the French classicists might have avoided getting themselves into this tight box if they had paid less attention to the later critics, even to Voltaire himself, and if they had gone back to Corneille, the father of French tragedy. Corneille was a born playwright, if ever there was one, with an instinctive apprehension of the principles of playmaking. He was a very mitigated classicist; in fact, he was plainly a classicist against his will and only in consequence of the strictures of the French Academy on his earliest masterpiece, the 'Cid.' In his third 'Discourse on Dramatic Art' Corneille showed a clear understanding of the principle which Horace had declared. "The poet is not obliged to put on the stage all the subsidiary actions which bring about the main action; he ought to choose those which are most advantageous to be seen, from the beauty of the spectacle or from the vigor and the vehemence of the passions which they produce, or from any other advantage they may have. And he ought to hide the others off the stage, letting them become known to the spectator either by a narration or by some other device of the art."

Here, with intuitive certainty, Corneille laid his finger on the reasons why certain parts of the story should be shown in action,—those which are interesting to the audience "from the vigor and the vehemence of the passions they produce." Here he was anticipating Robert Louis Stevenson's assertion that the drama is most dramatic when it sets before the spectators the great passionate crises of existence, "when duty and inclination come nobly to the grapple." Here, he was justifying in advance Brunetière's Law that the stuff out of which drama can be made most effectively, is the stark assertion of the human will and the collision of contending desires. Here, once more, he was on the verge of discovering Sarcey's most significant contribution to the theory of the theater,—that in any story there are certain episodes, interviews, moments, which the spectator must see for himself and which if not shown will leave the audience dumbly disappointed by their absence. Sarcey called these the scenes that must be shown, the *scènes à faire;* and Mr. William Archer has called them the Obligatory Scenes.

There is no characteristic of the born playwright more obvious than this,—that he makes an immediate and an unerring choice between the Obligatory Scenes, which the spectators will expect to have placed before their eyes, and the less significant parts of the plot, as to which the audience is quite willing to be informed "either by a narrative or by some other device of the art." In the drama, as in all the other departments of poetry, the half is often greater than the whole. Indeed, since the Middle Ages the dramatist has never sought to put on the stage all the details of his story; he has felt himself forced to make a choice and to focus the attention of the audience upon the moments which are really worth while.

IV

In the first of his 'Discourses on Dramatic Art,' Corneille had plaintively remarkt, "It is certain that there are Laws of the drama, since it is an art; but it is not certain what these laws are." And even when we have good reason to believe that we have at last laid hold of an indisputable principle, we can never be quite assured as to its proper application. Horace advised the avoidance of the offensively horrible;

> Let not Medea kill her boys in view.

For the reasons already suggested the Greeks had to refrain from the exhibition of any murder, altho they seem to have had a mechanical device for bringing into view the gory corpse after the victim had been slain behind closed doors. The French, governed by the decorum of the court of Louis XIV, were content that all scenes of murderous violence should be left to

> The actor's well-graced speech to tell.

But we who speak English do not

> Turn away in sceptical disgust

when Richard and Richmond cross swords or
when Macbeth and Macduff at last stand face to
face to fight to the death. Nor are we revolted
by the murder of Desdemona, painful tho it is
to witness, nor by the suicide of Othello. To
some of us, no doubt, there comes a feeling of
satiety, in the last act of 'Hamlet,' when the stage
is littered with the bodies of character after
character removed from this life by battle, murder
and sudden death; and there are other plays of
Shakspere's at the performance of which some of
us are a little annoyed by the prodigality of assassination. We are well aware that this or that
character is doomed to die; but we would not
object if we were spared from beholding the deep
damnation of his taking off and if his necessary
demise had been made known to us "either by a
narrative or by some other device of the art."

It is because Æschylus and Shakspere were
born playwrights, masters of all the devices of
the art, that they were each of them enabled to
move us more powerfully by an unseen murder,
by an assassination behind closed doors, than
we could have been moved if we had been forced
to see the fatal stroke descend and the smitten
victim drop. In the 'Agamemnon' we know
that Clytemnestra has gone within, resolved to
slay the husband who had wronged her and whom
she has wronged, and we listen in dread suspense,
not daring to hope that she will abandon her
deadly purpose; we wait until we hear the wail-

ing outcry of the betrayed hero, taken unawares and treacherously stricken in his own house. The only other moment in all drama which surpasses this in thick intensity of expectant horror is that when Macbeth, goaded by the stern purpose of his ambitious wife, takes up the daggers and creeps into the inner chamber where Duncan, his king and his guest, lies sleeping the sleep from which he is never to awaken. It is the outcry of Agamemnon which tells us that he has been slain; and Duncan makes no outcry. We know that he has been slain only when Macbeth comes out from the room which he entered a brave man and which he leaves a craven from that time on. That an unseen murder, which we are made to feel impending and inevitable, is more effective dramatically we discover when in the same play we are witnesses of the later assassination of Banquo, which discloses itself merely a brutal and vulgar slaughter, devoid of horror and of terror.

Jules Lemaitre once wrote a criticism of Maeterlinck's tragedy of childhood, the 'Death of Tintagiles'; and he began by quoting Horace's

> Whate'er's transmitted thru the ear
> To mind and heart will never come so near
> As what is set before the eyes, and each
> Spectator sees, brought full within his reach.

Then the brilliant French critic declared that "this is true,—and yet it is not true. Yes, often, what is set before our eyes, strikes us more forcibly than what is merely told; yes, action is ordinarily more moving than narrative. But what is infinitely more pathetic than an action told or seen, is an action which is divined. Victor Hugo has said that nothing is more interesting than a wall behind which something is taking place." And here Lemaitre and Hugo suggest to us the explanation why the deaths of Agamemnon and Duncan, which happened out of our sight behind a wall, are more moving than if we had seen them with our own eyes, because in each case we divine the dire event about to happen beyond our vision. Lemaitre remarkt that he found this blank wall in play after play of Maeterlinck's; and he discovered also in Maeterlinck an unfailing power of forcing us to divine what was taking place behind the wall. Poor little Tintagiles had fled up the stairs of the tower till he comes to an iron gate. His feeble voice calls for his sister, whom we see trying in vain to open the gate. At last, we hear the sound of the little body falling on the far side of the door. "And this is terrible, because we have seen nothing, not the child shivering with fright, not her who is not ever named, the wicked old woman whose hundred year old hands strangle the child so slowly that he has time to glue his mouth to the iron bars."

Plainly enough when Horace asserts that what is heard is less effective than what is seen and when the old stager bids the novice to "show everything important and let the spectators see it themselves," they have neither of them been able to do more than draft a rough-and-ready Rule, which is true and yet not true. They have not succeeded in laying firm hold on a principle so certain that it is true in all cases, indisputable and inexorable.

V

FOR example, that is a sound Rule which bids the playwright not to keep a secret from the audience. Bronson Howard once told me that the one of the dullest evenings he ever spent in the theater was due to the playwright's having hidden from the spectators the actual facts, thus putting them upon a false trail. The play was a dramatization of Miss Braddon's novel 'Henry Dunbar,' made by Tom Taylor. A daughter knows that her father has been wronged by Henry Dunbar and has been led thereby into a life of crime. She receives a letter from her father announcing his intention of seeking Henry Dunbar (who has just returned to England after a long stay in India), and of having it out with his old enemy. And after that she hears nothing more from her father, who has vanisht from the face of the earth. She has no doubt that Henry Dunbar has made away with him; so she sets out in pursuit. But Henry Dunbar evades her again and again, just when they are on the point of meeting. At last she corners him; and in the Henry Dunbar who

18

stands at bay before her she recognizes her father—who has killed his enemy and assumed that enemy's name and that enemy's fortune. The disclosure is effective, in its way; it procures a shock of surprise; but the total effect is far less than it would have been if the spectator had known the facts from the first. In that case there would have been no shock of surprise, but there would have been a steadily increasing intensity of suspense as the daughter came nearer to the father whom she loved and whom she was to find an assassin.

In Lessing's implacable dissection of Voltaire's 'Merope,' he admits that "our surprise is greater if we do not know with certainty that Ægisthus is Ægisthus before Merope knows it. But what a poor amusement is this surprise! And why need the poet surprise us? He may surprise his characters as much as he likes; and we shall derive our pleasure therefrom, even if we have long foreseen what befals them so unexpectedly. Nay, our sympathy will be the more vivid and the more vigorous, the longer and more certainly we have foreseen it. . . . Let the characters knot the complication without knowing it; let it be impenetrable for them; let it bring them without their foreknowledge nearer and nearer to the untying. If the characters feel emotion, the spectators will yield to the same feelings."

When Lessing wrote this he was a bold man,

for he was confessing a heresy. He records his dissent from the Rule laid down by a majority of those who had written on the dramatic art and who insisted that the spectators should be kept guessing at the final solution, never permitted to foresee it. Even so practical a playwright as Lope de Vega held that it was wise to conceal the way in which the plot was to be wound up, so that the audience might not be tempted to get up and go out as soon as the end of the complication became visible. Voltaire, also a practical playwright, thought that Sophocles should have kept the spectators of his 'Œdipus' in an ignorance of the secret as total as that which envelopt the characters. It was only toward the middle of the nineteenth century that Sophocles began to be praised for the very quality for which he had been blamed in the eighteenth.

What was flagrant heresy in the eighteenth century is accepted as establisht dogma in the twentieth century. Yet even today the Rule that a secret must not be kept from the audience is only a rule-of-thumb. It is not one of the permanent principles of playmaking; and a dextrous dramatist may sometimes see his profit in breaking the Rule, if by so doing he can achieve what appears to him an intensification of emotional interest. Paul Hervieu called one of his pieces the 'Enigma'; and he concealed from the spectators almost up to the falling of the final curtain which of two sisters had been guilty of admitting a detected lover by night; but it may be doubted whether the result of his experiment proved it to be justified. Perhaps he would have heightened his appeal if we had known from the beginning which was the guilty wife. "By means of secrecy," said Lessing, "a poet effects a short surprize, but in what an enduring disquietude he could have maintained us if he had made no secret about it! Whoever is struck down in a moment, I can pity only for a moment. But how if I expect the blow?—How if I can see the storm brewing and threatening for some time over the head of a character?"

None the less are there occasions where the Rule has to be broken, in the interest of the play as a whole,—that is to say, in the interest of the spectators themselves. In 'Henry Dunbar' the Rule not to keep a secret from the spectators was violated to the disadvantage of the play. But in Bronson Howard's own piece, 'Young Mrs. Winthrop,' it was violated to the advantage of the play,—and it was deliberately violated, so its author told me, because it conflicted with one of the eternal principles of playmaking. Young Mrs. Winthrop is jealous because her husband is frequently visiting a woman whose antecedents are doubtful. This brings about a dispute so violent that Mrs. Winthrop leaves her husband's house. In the final act, she learns that her suspicions were unfounded, since her husband's visits to her supposed rival were due to a highly honorable motive. But the author had kept this motive a secret from the spectators and had allowed them to believe that the jealousy of the wife was probably justified. When I askt him why he had done this, he explained that he needed to have his audience sympathize with his heroine when she left her husband and that the spectators must see things thru her eyes and believe the worst. Having only the information that the wife had, they would feel that her departure from her husband's home was fully warranted. If they had known that the husband was innocent of any wrongdoing they would have credited their own knowledge to the wife and they would have held her to be unreasonable if she broke with him for a suspicion which they had seen to be unfounded. And in this case, the spectators did not resent having been kept in the dark, for they were not formally told that Winthrop was guilty,—they were merely left in doubt; and therefore they were ready enough to be pleased when he was relieved from suspicion and reunited to his wife.

VI

THAT it is unsafe to pin faith to the Rules which happen to be current in our own time and to feel confident that they contain the law and the gospel was made manifest in the first half of the second decade of the twentieth century, when there happened to be produced in New York half-a-dozen plays characterized by an honest effort to find new methods of expression and to broaden the scope of theatrical presentation. In 'A Poor Little Rich Girl' the spectators were made to see scenes and characters that existed only in the ignorant imaginings of a child in the grip of fever. In 'Seven Keys to Baldpate' the clever author played a characteristically clever trick upon the audience itself, most unexpectedly taking them into his workshop. In 'On Trial' we were invited to behold in three successive acts, events which took place long before the beginning of the play itself, and the event thus shown in the second act was earlier than that shown in the first act and the event shown in the third act was earlier than that shown in the second,—thus taking us further and further backward toward the beginning of the story. In the 'Phantom Rival' we had presented before us the fond day-dreams of a fanciful woman,—day-dreams made actually visible to us, forced to take on a concrete existence, and peopled by four contradictory possibilities of a single character, creations called into life only by the brooding imagination of the heroine. And in the 'Big Idea' we were invited to witness the successive

23

steps of the invention, the construction, and the
writing of a play, which is to be built on the
dangerous predicament in which the chief character finds himself in the piece which is actually
being performed; and this big idea is carried so
far that at last we discover that the play which has
been put together before our eyes is the very
play which is being performed before our eyes.

In all these dramas, serious, comic and serio-
comic, four of them American in authorship and
one of them freely Americanized from a Hungarian
original, there was a deliberate intention to
achieve novelty of form. They were all characterized by ingenuity of invention; and at least
two of them can be credited, more or less, with the
loftier quality of imagination. They might be
termed new departures in the drama, due to the
desire of their several authors to desert the beaten
path and to explore fresh fields. They were all
of them more or less successful on the stage; that
is to say, the authors were able to carry the public
with them along these hitherto untrodden trails.
Indeed, it may as well be admitted that a consider-
able share of the popularity of these pieces was
directly due to the attraction exerted upon the
spectator by the freshness of treatment which is
their most salient quality. These plays seemed
to not a few among those who discuss the drama
to prove that the wisest of men was less wise than
was his wont when he insisted that there was

nothing new under the sun. And the favorable reception of this series of daring experiments in stagecraft was the more surprising since the theater itself has always been considered ultra-conservative, clinging desperately to ancient landmarks, and struggling blindly against all efforts to overturn its traditions and to over-throw its customs.

There is no occasion for surprize, therefore, that we should have been told vehemently and vociferously that all the traditions of the theater were to be abandoned, that all the customs of the stage were to be renounced, that all the Rules of the Drama were hereafter to be broken, that all the Laws hitherto held binding upon the playwright were to be repealed, and that all the principles of playmaking were suddenly reduced to chaotic confusion. To many ardent aspirants for drama-turgic victory it seemed almost as if a bomb had been suddenly exploded in the temple of the drama, shattering the tables of the law and bring-ing down the walls in ruin. A skilful and success-ful American playwright was quoted as asserting that "the day is not far distant when there will be no stage conventions, so far as the audience is concerned." A newspaper reviewer of current plays felt emboldened to declare that the profes-sor of dramatic literature in one of our leading universities must be greatly grieved by the success of one of the five plays already cited—a play writ-

ten by one of the professor's former students—
because it violated all the doctrines about the
drama, which the professor had been discussing
year after year.

Now, if this happened to be true, and if the
public should accept a play which violated the
theories to which this professor of dramatic
literature had drawn the attention of his classes,
then this would go far toward disestablishing the
validity of these theories and it would put the professor in a situation so awkward as to demand
explanation, if not apology to all his former pu-
pils. But fortunately for this professor these
assertions as to the complete upsetting of the
doctrines hitherto expounded by those who have
sought to penetrate into the secrets of stagecraft,
were not well founded. They were the result of
a failure to perceive the wide distinction between
the Rules and the Laws which had won acceptance
for the moment and the eternal principles of playmaking, which are unchanging because they are
essential to the existence of the art.

VII

SINCE the five plays in which there were novelties of construction succeeded in pleasing the
playgoers, it is safe to say that no one of them
violated any of the eternal principles of playmaking. But did any one of them really contradict

any of the generally accepted Precepts of the contemporary theater?

It is difficult to see any reason why anybody should suppose that either the 'Poor Little Rich Girl,' or the 'Phantom Rival,' broke any of the Rules, unexpected as might be their calling upon the spectator to behold things that exist only in the imagination of one of the characters— things that did not happen actually but which that character merely believed to be happening. The authors of these two plays were skilful and careful; they made elaborate preparation; they led us forward step by step; they told us what they were going to do, what they were doing, and what they had done. They were so clear and so straightforward that they compel us to follow them. What they askt us to accept might be very unusual and in itself not easy to accept; but they so presented it that it was not difficult for us to accept. After all, the sole novelty lay in their asking us to witness what happened in a day-dream, just as a host of earlier playwrights had invited the playgoer of the past to behold what happened in a dream. The 'Victorine' of four score years ago was not the earliest of dream-plays and the 'Romance' of more recent years will not be the last. In the 'Phantom Rival' and the 'Poor Little Rich Girl' the actual novelty was not as new as it may have appeared to the younger generation of playgoers; and the authors had not needed to break any of the traditional Precepts of the theater.

The authors of 'Seven Keys to Baldpate' and of the 'Big Idea' were equally mindful of the principles of the art, and they did not try to "fool the audience." In the 'Big Idea,' which was the more daring of the two amusing dramas, the authors took the spectator into their confidence from the beginning. We were made to see the hero and the heroine start to write the very play in which they are characters. The device was dangerous, and difficult of acceptance; but the successive scenes were so clear and they were so logically related, each growing out of its predecessor, naturally and irresistibly, that we could not help surrendering ourselves to the delight of watching the authors win their wager. Here again, we were told what they were going to do, what they were doing, and what they had done. Even the appeal of the heroine in the final act directly and personally to the assembled audience asking it to like the play which had been put together before its eyes and in which she was a character—even this was not the flagrant novelty that it may have seemed to some. Its most immediate predecessor is to be found in 'Peter Pan,' but it is a device for evoking laughter, which Molière employed in the 'Miser' and Aristophanes in the 'Frogs.'

There still remains to be considered 'On Trial,'

which was hailed as the most subversive of all these plays, since "it told its story backward." If 'On Trial' had told its story backward, it would have broken the Rule which prescribes that a playwright must devise an action with a beginning, a middle and an end, and that he must present these several parts in strict sequence. But, as a matter of fact, the author of 'On Trial' did not tell its story backward; he told it straight forward, altho he took the liberty of showing us in successive acts fragments of his story which had taken place before the moment when he had chosen to begin it. His play set before us a man on trial for his life. The scene of every act was laid in the court-room, with the judge on the bench, the prisoner at the bar, the jury in the box and the opposing counsel. In the first act, the widow of the murdered man was called to the witness stand and she began to give her testimony, when suddenly there was a dark change and we were made to see in action the episode as to which she was about to testify; and when we had seen this, then there was another dark change, after which we found her on the stand finishing her testimony. In the second act, the little daughter of the prisoner was called as a witness; and again we were made spectators of the events as to which she was supposed to be testifying. In the third act when the wife of the prisoner was summoned to the stand, we were once more invited to be spectators of the thing itself instead of being merely listeners to her testimony. If these three witnesses had been allowed to give their evidence in their own words, no one would have suggested that the story was being told backward, because every playgoer knows that in every play there are events which happened long before the play began and which can be made known to the audience only by a telling after the event has happened. The author of 'On Trial' did not break any of the Rules; he was merely inventive enough and ingenious enough to devise a new way of making visible to us in the present what had taken place in the past. The novelty was in the method of presentation and not in any departure from the Precepts generally accepted in the theater.

(1914–16.)

II

HOW TO WRITE A PLAY

I

THE title of this paper may seem presumptuous. Who am I that I should presume to proffer instruction in the art of the playwright, as difficult as it is dangerous? If this hurrying twentieth century of ours were only the leisurely eighteenth century, when everybody had all the time there was, a fit name for this paper might be: "A few tentative Suggestions for those who propose to commence Playwrights, garnered from the Experience of an old Playgoer." That may be a more accurate, as it is a more cautious, description of the intent of the present paper; but it is a little too long drawn to serve as a title for an article on a topic of immediate interest to an immense number of ambitious aspirants.

It has been calculated by an imaginative statistician that there are now in these United States nearly one hundred thousand persons—men, women and children—who are eager to write plays, believing that the stage door is the easiest entrance to the Temple of Fortune and to the

Hall of Fame. Whether or not this estimate is scientifically accurate may not be disclosed even when we have the figures of the new census. Quite possibly it is not at all inflated, since it allows only one apprentice playmaker to every thousand of the population. At all events, there are so many of them that advertisements have appeared of late addressed especially to those ignorant of dramatic art and yet ambitious to acquire it. "Playwriting Taught by Mail" is an alluring temptation which is probably charming subscriptions from the pockets of many an eager youth.

Whether or not playwriting can really be taught by mail is a question that need not here be discust. What is not a question is that it can be taught, even if these advertisers may not be capable of teaching it. Playwriting is an art and every art must be learnt; and whatever must be learned can be taught—whether it is the art of painting a portrait, of riming a lyric, of making a speech or of writing a play. It is true that the poet is born, not made; but it is also true that after he is born he has to be made. What he has to say may be the gift of God, but how he is to say it depends upon the training of the bard himself. In every artist we can perceive a man with both a message and a method. His message may be innate in him, but his method he has to acquire from others. The painters have recognized this; and they promptly go to school to the older practitioners of the craft that they may imbibe its secrets and be shown how to set a palette and how to bring out on the canvas before them the things they see in the world around them. Every painter is the pupil of one or more painters of an earlier generation; and he is proud of it as a proof that he has served his apprenticeship and learnt his trade properly.

Whatever has to be learnt can be taught; but it can be taught best by those who have practised it themselves. The instructors in the art schools are painters, not art critics or historians of art. And, if playwriting is to be taught with the same success that painting has been taught, this can be accomplisht only by the older playwrights instructing the younger and laying bare before them the art and mystery of the drama. If a school of playwriting were to be opened the proper instructors would be Mr. Gillette and Mr. Augustus Thomas in the United States, and Sir Arthur Pinero and Mr. Henry Arthur Jones in Great Britain. In France, more than half-a-century ago, there was for a while something very like a school of playwriting kept by a master play-wright, Scribe—that is to say, Scribe liked to collaborate and he was hospitable to the young men who brought him suggestions for plays. He showed these young men how their suggestions could be turned to profit on the stage. And in this collaboration the young men could not fail to get an insight into Scribe's method and to discover some of the reasons why Scribe's plays were incessantly reappearing in all the theaters of Europe.

And yet a mere critic, a mere historian of the drama, may on occasion be able to proffer advice, not so much to the point, perhaps, as would be that of the successful playwright, but not without a certain value of its own, however inferior. When anyone has been intensely interested in the drama for more than forty years, and when he has been an assiduous playgoer in many cities, and when he has taken advantage of every opportunity to discuss the problems of playmaking with the many dramatists he has had the good fortune to count among his friends—it may not be unreasonable for him to assume that it is in his power to call attention to a few of the more obvious points which the ambitious young dramatic author must ever bear in mind. He may not be justified in advertising "Playwriting Taught by Mail," but he ought to be able to make a few elementary suggestions.

The first of these obvious considerations for the benefit of the 'prentice playwright is that he ought to devote himself to playgoing. Nearly forty years ago, when I hoped that I might become a professional playwright, I introduced myself to the late Eugène Nus, the author of the French originals of Charles Reade's 'Hard Cash,'

Boucicault's 'Streets of New York,' and Tom
Taylor's 'Ticket-of-Leave Man.' Tho the play
plotted as a result of this introduction was
never actually written, one remark of the veteran
French playmaker may be recalled: "Young
man, if you want to write for the theater you must
go to the theater." Every writer of plays must
be intimately familiar with the theater of his own
time and his own country, since that is the only
theater where he can hope to have his plays produced. He must understand its organization and
its mechanism. He must study earnestly not only
the theater itself but the actors—and, above all,
the audiences.

He must go to see the successful plays of the
season again and again, in the endeavor to discover the causes of their success and the means
whereby this success has been attained. The
first time he is a spectator at the performance of
a play he is likely to be merely a spectator—carried
away like the rest of the audience by the story
itself, by the interest of the plot, by the excite-
ment of the successive episodes. When he gets
home he will do well to analize his impressions
and to ask himself how it was that these impressions were produced. Then he will do well to go
again to verify this analysis and to clear up the
points that may have been left in doubt. At
this second visit he ought to be able to perceive a
little more clearly the method of the author—

the reasons, for example, why a certain interview is in the fourth act and not in the third; and the reasons why certain parts of the story are shown in action and certain other parts are merely narrated or otherwise explained to the audience. He ought to note especially how the dramatist has conveyed to the spectators the information about what has happened before the play began, not necessary to be shown in action and yet absolutely necessary if the actual story is to be followed with understanding.

Then he may go a third time—and a fourth—until he has mastered the construction of the play; whereupon he may turn his attention from the play to the audience, marking when the spectators are fidgety and when they are swept along by the resistless rush of the action. When he perceives that some of the audience are looking at their programs, or whispering to their neighbors, he had better look again at the play to discover, if he can, what made the interest relax at that moment.

Nor should he neglect the failures and devote himself wholly to the successes. Many an interesting lesson can be derived from a failure. The student can at least try to ascertain why it failed. He can let it teach him what to avoid. He can watch the behavior of the scant audience; and this will sometimes be as illuminating as the conduct of the spectators at a successful play. Every dramatist, the mightiest as well as the less signi-

36

ficant—Shakspere and Molière, no less than Sardou and Belasco—has always kept his eye on his audience. If he does not desire above all things to interest and to move and to hold the audience, then he has no business with playwriting.

It is his first duty to find out what the playgoers of his own time and his own country enjoy, for that is what he will have to give them in his plays—even if he may be able also to give them something more. When he has learned this art he may express himself and deliver his own message—if he has one; but he has always to keep his audiences in mind and to remember that they have to be interested in the play, or his message will never reach its destination. He has to feel with his spectators, so that he may make them feel with him. This does not mean any "writing down to the vulgar mob"; but it does mean "writing broad for the people as a whole."

'Hamlet,' for example, is Shakspere's masterpiece, rich in poetry and lofty in philosophy; but it is also a very amusing play for the gallery-boy, who cares little either for poetry or for philosophy, but who is delighted by the ghost, by the-play within-the-play and by the duel with the poisoned swords. It has been asserted that if 'Hamlet' should be performed in a deaf-and-dumb asylum the inmates would be able to follow the story with interest by means of their eyes alone. A wise critic once declared that the skeleton of a good play is a pantomime. 'Tartuffe' for example is Molière's masterpiece, a marvelously rich portrayal of human nature; and it has a pantomime for its backbone. When the Comédie-Française went to London, forty years ago, Sarcey picked out 'Tartuffe' as the one play of all the repertory that produced the most certain effect upon the English playgoers, since its story was so clear that it could be followed even by those ignorant of French.

If the successful play of the hour happens to be publisht the aspirant will do well to get it and to compare the impression he had in the theater itself with that made by the printed page in the library. This will help to show him how much of the effect of a play is due to the performance—to the acting, to the looks and gestures, to the pauses and to the sense of suspense. And it will probably startle him to discover how little of the effect is due to external literary merit, to mere writing, to rhetoric; and how much of this effect is the result of the story itself, of the building up of the situations so that one seems to arise naturally out of another; and of the bold, sharp contrast of character with character. "Fine writing" is nowadays at a discount; and in the theater action is all important. This is no new discovery, for Aristotle said it many centuries ago, insisting that story and construction were absolutely necessary, whereas poetry was only a decoration or an accompaniment. A good play must have literary merit, of course; but it must be drama before it is literature. It has to succeed on the stage or it will never be read.

The ambitious aspirant will find advantage, also, in analizing contemporary publisht plays that he has not seen acted and in trying to guess at their effectiveness in the theater. Sardou once told a reporter how he had studied Scribe's pieces in the endeavor to spy out the secrets of stage-craft. "I used to take a three-act play that I did not know anything about. I read only the first act; and, after this exposition of the story and of the characters, I closed the book and then I tried to build up for myself the rest of the play that Scribe had erected on that foundation. And I was satisfied with myself only when I had, by a sheer exercise of logic, succeeded in constructing a plot pretty close to that which I afterward found in the second and third acts." Scribe is now a little old-fashioned; but today a novice would find it very suggestive if he took Pinero's 'Mid-Channel,' Jones' 'Liars,' or Clyde Fitch's 'Girl with the Green Eyes,' and, after studying the first act very carefully, tried to outline the play that is the necessary conclusion.

To say this is to emphasize the fact that the art of the dramatist is very like the art of the architect. A plot has to be built up just as a house is built—story after story; and no edifice has any chance of standing unless it has a broad foundation and a solid frame. What the characters say is less important than what they do, and still less important than what they are. After the steel frame is once erected there will be time enough to consider the decoration and to design the stained-glass windows. The story, the plot, the theme—these are the essential things. Voltaire says somewhere that the success of a play depends on the choice of its subject. And whether a subject is good or not depends on the audience. Subjects that were excellent for Sophocles and for Shakspere are no longer satisfactory to modern spectators, who have a very different outlook on the world from that of the Athenians or the Elizabethans. The spectator today wants to see himself on the stage—himself and his fellows— the kind of folks he knows by personal experience. And it is only by choosing a subject of this sort that the novice can give his work what the late Augustin Daly used to call "contemporaneous human interest."

A play needs to have a theme; this theme must be interpreted by a story; and the story must be stiffened into a plot. The plot may be simple and straightforward, free from complications and complexities; but it must deal with a struggle. It must show the clash of contending desires. This marks the sharp difference between the novel and the play. Alone in the library we are often glad to read a novel which sets before us merely a group of characters, revealing themselves by word of mouth; but in the theater, when we are assembled together, we are bored if we are not shown a definite action, a steadily moving story in which we can follow the strife of opposing forces. A novel may delight us by merely exhibiting human beings; but a play is not likely to please us unless we can sympathize with the effort of one of those human beings to attain a definite purpose. On the stage we want to see somebody wanting something and either getting it or not getting it. We want to see a fight, fought to the finish.

When Mr. Gillette set out to put Sherlock Holmes into a play he instinctively seized upon the shadowy figure of Professor Moriarty, the astute leader of a band of criminals—a figure only glimpst vaguely in a far corner of one of the least known of Sir Arthur Conan Doyle's stories. Mr. Gillette put this figure in the forefront of the play he was composing, and set him over against the incomparable detective, thus providing Sherlock Holmes with a foeman worthy of his steel. The resulting play was a duel of wits between the wrong embodied in Moriarty and the right personified by Sherlock Holmes. And a very large part of the success of the 'Lion and the Mouse' was due to the ease with which the audience was able to follow the bitter contention between the heroine and the plutocrat, each of them knowing his own mind and each of them feeling justified in his own conscience. It may be noted, also, that the 'Taming of the Shrew' is one of the least intellectual of Shakspere's plays, it is primarily a farce, with an abundance of violent fun; but it keeps the stage after three centuries because its story is vigorously dramatic, since it sets before us an unmistakable contention of opposing forces, resulting in the conquest of a woman's will by a man's.

One piece of advice to the novice can properly be offered by a student of stage history. Begin modestly. Begin by imitating the successful playwrights of your own time and your own country. Be satisfied, at first, if you can succeed in doing only what these predecessors have done—even if you believe you have it in you to do better. Don't try to be precocious. As Margaret Fuller said: "For precocity some great price is always demanded sooner or later in life." The great dramatists have never exhibited any undue precocity; they have always begun modestly by imitating. Shakspere's earliest pieces are merely his juvenile attempts to write the kind of play that Marlowe and Kyd, Lyly and Greene had made popular. Molière's earliest plays are imitations of the improvised comedies of the Italian strollers. In these early efforts of Shakspere and Molière it is scarcely possible to perceive even the promise of the power to which they ultimately attained. Henry Arthur Jones began by writing comediettas and melodramas; and Sir Arthur Pinero made an equally unambitious beginning with curtain-raisers.

The really important dramatist is, of course, a man who has something to say and who has learnt how to say it. In his immaturity he is not likely to have much to say of any great significance; and he can, therefore, concentrate his attention on learning how to say what little he has to utter. An anecdote is told of Courbet, the French painter, which brings out this point. A very ambitious young fellow came to him for advice, enlarging upon the lofty projects he had in mind. Courbet listened and then answered: "Go home and paint a portrait of your father." The young man protested at this humble task, proclaiming his desire to paint great historical scenes. "Exactly," said Courbet, "I understand—you want to become a historical painter. That is why I tell you to go home and paint a portrait of your father."

This is excellent advice for beginners in every art. Like the aviators, they must be content to fly along the level ground for a little distance before they attempt to soar aloft into the blue empyrean.

(1911.)

III

ON PUTTING LITERATURE INTO THE DRAMA

I

WHEN the future historian of the American drama comes to deal with the final years of the nineteenth century and the early years of the twentieth, he will do well to record that the riper development in that period was retarded by three untoward events,—the premature deaths of Clyde Fitch and William Vaughan Moody and the premature birth of Bronson Howard.

Moody was a poet who was engaged in conscientiously acquiring the art of the playwright when his career was cut short; and if he had lived we should have had a right to reckon on a series of serious plays deep in purpose and expert in craftsmanship—plays in which we should find a fulfilment of the expectations aroused by the promising 'Great Divide' and 'Faith Healer.' Clyde Fitch ran a longer course; he was far more prolific; and he had to his credit half-a-dozen or half-a-score popular successes. But there was no one of his plays which sustained its entire action on the high level he had been able to attain in separate scenes when he was at his best. The third act of the 'Girl with the Green Eyes' was a masterpiece of dramaturgic skill and of psychologic veracity, but it was followed by a fourth act so inept as to be beneath contempt. The Duke in the 'Coronet of the Duchess' was a vital character created with real insight into human nature, but the play itself was false in motive and feeble in construction. Fitch was honestly ambitious; and he believed to the end that his best work was still before him.

As both Moody and Fitch were taken from us before they had achieved their full artistic maturity, we cannot even guess what ampler effort they might have put forth if they had been spared. But we can see that there was a definite loss to the American drama in the appearance of Bronson Howard a score of years too early. He had an unusual endowment for dramatic authorship; he had the instinct for theatrical effect; he had a keen sense of character; he had an individual insight into human nature; he had an intuitive understanding of the fundamental principles of playmaking; and he had a broad outlook on life. But he came to maturity and he did his best work in a period of rapid transition,—in the years before the artificial methods of Sardou and of Boucicault had been supplanted by the sterner simplicity of Ibsen and of the host of latter-day playwrights who responded to the stimulus of Ibsen's masterly technic. The overt theatricality of the playmakers of half-a-century ago has now fallen into disrepute, for we expect today to find in our more ambitious dramas a less arbitrarily arranged story, a theme of more vital interest, handled with a more obvious veracity. We demand a more serious treatment of motive and an ampler vision of life.

These qualities we do not find in Bronson Howard's plays, clever as they were and amusing as they were. We cannot help confessing that they seem to us compounded according to an outworn formula. Their merits, undeniable as they are, strike us now as ingeniously theatrical rather than truly dramatic. These pieces were good in their own day; but they are not good enough to withstand the change in our standards. They are unfortunately old-fashioned, even if we can still admire the power and the felicity with which certain episodes are handled, like that in 'Shenandoah,' where the soldier father all unwittingly conducts the funeral of his unrecognized son, a scene which is a little masterpiece of unforced pathos. And the reason why these successful plays, the 'Banker's Daughter,' 'Young Mrs. Winthrop' and the 'Henrietta' are out-of-date today is that they were up-to-date yesterday; they are what they are because their author conformed to the customs of his youth. But those

who knew Bronson Howard personally can testify that he had it in him to write plays of a finer
substance and of a solider truth than he was
permitted to write in the changing epoch when he
was at work. He was subdued to what he workt
in; and he was born out of time. If he had come
into this world forty years later he would have
employed the simpler methods which are now
acceptable; he would have dealt more sincerely
with life; he would have been more truly dramatic
without surrendering his theatrical effectiveness;
he would have utilized more imaginatively his
persistent and inquisitive observation of conduct
and of character.

Most successful artists work rather by instinct
than by rule; they achieve their results more or
less unconscious of the laws they are obeying;
and only a very few can be trusted to analize
their own processes and to explain why they did
what they did in the way they did. Bronson
Howard was one of the small minority who could
always give a reason for the faith that was in him.
His methods were intuitive, of course, or they
would not have accomplisht the result at which
he was aiming; but they were also authenticated
by his constant reflection upon the principles of
playwriting. After he had been guided by his
intuition he could explain to himself the reason
why he had done what he had done. In other
words, he had strengthened his native instinct

47

by philosophic inquiry into the unvarying principles of playmaking.

II

THIS is a lengthy preamble to a brief anecdote. In the early eighties of the last century the Authors Club was founded in New York; and at its fortnightly gatherings men of letters came together for informal converse,—poets and playwrights, novelists and essayists, historians and philosophers. In their several degrees they were all makers of books, but they regarded literature each from his own special angle. The unexpected result of this interchange of view was a broadening of the outlook of those whose vision had been too narrowly focust on their own field of endeavor.

At one of these reunions I chanced to be the third of a group of which the other two were Bronson Howard and Richard Henry Stoddard, a poet who was inclined to take himself rather too seriously and who had little understanding of the drama. At a pause in our conversation Stoddard turned to Howard and put a question which seemed to me then, as indeed it does now, to be inspired by a combination of condescension and impertinence.

"Howard," he askt, "why don't you sometimes put a little literature into your pieces?"

The playwright was not at all disturbed by the unconscious discourtesy of this query.

"That is an easy question to answer," he replied. "I never *put* literature into my plays because I respect my art too much."

I doubt if Stoddard perceived the significance of the slight emphasis that Howard had given to the word *put*. He made no rejoinder; and our talk drifted to other topics.

Stoddard's inquiry revealed an attitude not uncommon among men of letters who take little interest in the theater and who are accustomed to consider the drama from the literary point of view. They think of a play as something intended only to be read—to be judged solely in the study and not also on the stage. What Stoddard sought in a play was "literary merit," so-called, that is to say, style, rhetoric, verbal brilliancy; he gave little heed to the more necessary merits of invention and construction. In his eyes "fine writing" made a fine play. It is because most of the poets of the English language took this view persistently in the nineteenth century that the English drama was then so sterile. Their attitude was not unfairly represented in the remark of Bayes in the 'Rehearsal,' when he inquired "What a Devil is the plot good for but to bring in fine things?" And by good things they meant glittering similes, pointed antitheses and an unending effulgence of figures of speech.

49

They would have had little sympathy with Joubert's incisive declaration that "what is wanted is not merely the poetry of images, but the poetry of ideas." They expected the dramatist to construct his decoration, feeling dissatisfied when he only decorated his construction.

The quarrel is ancient, if it is not honorable; and the men of letters could have pointed with pride to Seneca and to the Italians of the Renascence and to the French who followed in the footsteps of the Italians. But they would have found no support in the practice or in the precepts of the great Greek dramatists or of the great dramatists of the modern languages. The great dramatists know better than anyone else that plays do not live by style alone, but by substance, by invention and by construction, by imagination and by veracity. A good play must be well written, no doubt, but before it is written it must be well conceived and well developt; it must have a theme; it must have a story which reveals itself in a sequence of situations; and this plot must be peopled with human beings who look like human beings, who talk like human beings, and who act like human beings.

While the words by means of which these characters disclose themselves and carry on the action are important, they are far less important than the action itself. Moreover, true "literary merit" does not reside in the smoothness of the external rhetoric but in the vigorous harmony of the internal elements which enable the play to stand four-square to all the winds that blow. It is by the force of these internal elements that a drama maintains itself in the theater, even if it is more or less by its external charm of style that it pleases us also in the library. In the playhouse the play appeals to the playgoers, an incongruous mass made up of all sorts and conditions of men; yet the verdict of this mass is always sincere and it has always had the high respect of the great dramatists, who have indeed paid little or no regard to any other verdict. Probably most of the great dramatists would unhesitatingly subscribe to the assertion of one of the most adroit playwrights of our own time, Mr. William Gillette, when he declared that dramatic authors find the public "honest and straightforward with us always, ever ready to be moved by what is true and lifelike and human, provided it be made interesting; ever ready to reject the false and artificial, even tho it be festooned with literary gems."

"Festooned with literary gems!" Could there be an apter description of the "literature" that is *put* into a play, in the vain hope of disguising its falsity and its artificiality and of concealing its lack of truth and humanity? A dramatist who understands his art and respects it, never tries to put literature into his plays; he confines his effort to putting life into them, well aware that

if he achieves sincerity and veracity, he will also
attain literature without having strained for it.

III

THE overmastering desire to be "literary" on
all occasions and at all costs has wrecked the hopes
of many an ambitious man of letters when he
has sought success on the stage. Stevenson, for
example, believed that the artificiality of his
'Deacon Brodie,' its falsity to life, could be atoned
for by its sheer verbal beauty. He was able to
give his story this external merit; but he neg-
lected to give it the necessary internal merit of
sincerity. He amused himself by playing with
his subject, instead of wrestling with it after
fasting and prayer. He tried to palm off on the
public a verbal veneer as a substitute for the
solid mahogany which the public expected.
Clever as he was, he failed to see that a living
drama depends upon a stark simplicity of structure, which may admit of decoration but which
does not demand this, because it has ever the
undeniable beauty of perfect design, a beauty
equally undeniable even when it is unadorned.

Voltaire was a man of letters, beyond all question, but he was also a man with a wide and varied
experience in the theater; and it was this experience which once led him to set forth the essential
qualities of a play: "Compact a lofty and in-

teresting event in the space of two or three hours; bring forward the several characters only when each ought to appear; never leave the stage empty; develop a plot as probable as it is attractive; say nothing unnecessary; instruct the mind and move the heart; be eloquent always and with the eloquence proper to every character represented; use a language as pure as the most careful prose without permitting the fetters of rime to appear to interfere with the thought,—these are the conditions now imposed on tragedy." And if we strike out the injunction never to leave the stage empty and the advice about rime,—monitions of value only in French tragedy—we have here a characteristically penetrating analysis.

Man of letters as Voltaire was above all else, he did not ask the intending playwright to spend any of his energy on the effort to be "literary." Even when he prescribed the duty of being "eloquent always" he qualified this and explained his real meaning by adding "with the eloquence proper to every character represented." Plainly enough Voltaire was out of sympathy with the many poets of his own time who were wont to rely on "festoons of literary gems" and whose verbal glitter was often only pinchbeck and paste. With the same insight into the true conditions of dramatic composition, Voltaire, on another occasion, declared that tragedy welcomes metaphor and abhors simile. "Why? Because a metaphor, when it is natural, belongs to passion; but a simile belongs only to the intelligence."

When we consider the plays of Shakspere in the order in which he wrote them, it is interesting to see how he indulged freely in simile in the days of his apprenticeship to the art of playmaking; and how as he gained a firmer grasp on the principles of the art, he banisht simile and relied almost altogether upon metaphor. In 'Love's Labor's Lost,' for example, which is probably his earliest attempt at comedy, we can observe him joyfully displaying his own verbal dexterity, delighting in conceits and in fanciful comparisons, juggling with words for their own sake. Something of this he retained even when he wrote his youthful tragedy 'Romeo and Juliet,' where we can catch him in the act, so to speak, of "putting literature into a play." But there is nothing of this in the 'Macbeth' of his maturity; that achieves literature inevitably, by its simple veracity, and seemingly without overt exertion on his part. In 'Love's Labor's Lost' we can detect his own consciousness of his cleverness, whereas in 'Macbeth' he has ceased to be clever and is content to be true.

In nothing is Shakspere's ultimate mastery of his craft more clearly disclosed than in the unerring certainty with which he employed now prose and then blank verse as the varying episodes of his story seemed to demand the one or the other. In 'Julius Cæsar,' for instance, Brutus and Cassius and Mark Antony, the loftier figures of the tragedy, speak in blank verse; the less important characters make use of a rhythmic prose, effectively cadenced but lacking the rigorous restrictions of meter; the plebeians and the mob express their emotions and their opinions in bare prose.

Most of the modern poets of our language, when they have essayed a five-act tragedy, have failed to profit by Shakspere's example. They have not dared to drop into prose, even in dealing with the unpoetic commonplaces of everyday existence. They never cease to walk on stilts, because they are forever trying to put literature into their plays. "The ordinary English poetical play varies between rather slack and formless meter, and ornate, involved and ultra-poetical diction," so Professor Gilbert Murray asserts. "The first enables the poet to slide into prose when asking for his boots; the second, almost unassisted, has to keep up the poetic quality of the atmosphere. It does so, of course, at the expense of directness, and often with the ruinous result that where you have Drama you have killed Poetry, and where you have Poetry you have killed Drama."

IV

PROFESSOR MURRAY has here placed his finger on the prevailing defect of the English poetical play of the middle of the nineteenth century.

It insisted on being "poetical" at all times and at any cost. It was the result of a mistaken belief that a play could be made poetical by applying a varnish of "poetry." And a belief equally mistaken led the writers of English comedy of the same period to besprinkle their dialog with hand-made witticisms, with alleged epigrams, distributed lavishly to all the characters, even to the dullest and the least capable of making a joke. In the insubstantial comic pieces of H. J. Byron, anybody would say anything however inappropriate, to anybody else, if this could be made a cue for a cut-and-dried repartee. The spectators of these highly unreal pieces could not doubt that Byron kept a notebook in which he jotted down every joke, every quip and every pun that came to him; and they could almost see him taking out one or another of these merry jests to pin it into his dialog as best he could.

"The sure sign of a general decline of an art is the frequent occurence, not of deformity, but of misplaced beauty," said Macaulay with his customary common sense. "In general, tragedy is corrupted by eloquence and comedy by wit." Perhaps it is rather grandiloquence than actual eloquence which marks the decline of tragedy; but that comedy is debased by a perpetual questing of epigram, falsely so-called, must be admitted at once. The disappearance of the factitious and laborious "wit" from our more

56

recent plays is evidence that modern comedy is recovering its health.

Oscar Wilde was the latest British comic dramatist to indulge in incessant fireworks. But it is an error to suppose that his success on the stage was due to his scintillations and his corruscations. His best comedies are solidly built, with an ingenious story carefully elaborated into a compelling plot. The pleasure which we get from 'Lady Windemere's Fan' is only in small part derived from its varnish of witticisms, often highly arbitrary in themselves and sometimes very arbitrarily distributed. Indeed, there are already signs that the persistent and insistent crackle of the dialog is beginning to be annoying to latter-day audiences. We are losing our liking for an external dazzle which distracts our attention from the internal action artfully arranged to arouse and to retain out interest.

Even if 'Lady Windemere's Fan' is not quite sincere in its portrayal of character and not quite veracious in its dealing with life, it has an ingeniously articulated plot which would retain its potency even if the play should be translated into German and thence into Spanish and finally back into English,—an operation which would certainly brush off all the spangles that now glisten in the dialog. Yet we may be assured that these forced and fortuitous quips and quirks were not continuously injected because the author believed it to be his duty to put literature into his play, but rather because he recognized that he had to maintain his own reputation as a wit, as a manufacturer of cleverness, as a retailer of "good things." And it may be admitted that in bestowing this deliberate brilliance on his dialog, Wilde was dutifully following in the footsteps of the two masters of the English comedy of manners, Congreve and Sheridan.

In the third quarter of the nineteenth century the French drama also suffered from an epidemic of epigram. The foremost French comedy of that time, the 'Gendre de M. Poirier' of Augier and Sandeau, was more or less infected by this malady; and the chief rival of the 'Gendre de M. Poirier,' the 'Demi-Monde' of the younger Dumas, has been quarantined by later French critics because of its feverish eruption of witticisms. It is only fair to record that Dumas recovered, and that in his later 'Francillon' there is scarcely a single example of calculated repartee. The dialog of 'Francillon' seems spontaneous even when it is at its cleverest, whereas that of the 'Demi-Monde' strikes us today as mannered and metallic. The French playwrights of the twentieth century may even be accused of having reacted a little too violently from the practices of their immediate predecessors, since they appear almost to avoid wit.

So long as the dramatist, French, British or

American, was adjusting his plays to the apron-stage which brought the actors almost into personal contact with the audience and which invited the characters to be exuberantly grandiloquent in tragedy or confidentially witty in comedy, he was subject to a constant temptation to "put literature into the drama." But this temptation has diminisht, if it has not disappeared, now that our playwrights are all working for the picture-frame stage which keeps the actors far distant from the spectators and which therefore places a premium on simple and direct utterance.

(1918.)

IV

THREE THEORISTS OF THE THEATER

I

CRITICS of the drama are like the poor, in that they are always with us. It matters little whether the theater is flourishing or expiring; we are never at a loss for self-appointed judges, ready to pass condemnation on the principles and on the practices of the playwrights. In Alexandria when dramatic literature was nonexistent, as the glory that was Greece was slowly sinking out of sight, and in Italy again when there was a splendid renascence of all the arts save the drama alone, there existed a superabundant and superfluous host of critics, promulgating the rigid code which they had deduced from their own inner consciousness.

Indeed, it seems to be especially in times of dramatic penury that the theorists of the theater increase and multiply spontaneously. And this is most unfortunate, since it is quite as bad for a critic as it is for a poet to let himself lose sight of the actual playhouse, with its associated players and its accustomed playgoers. The fundamental principles of any art can be singled out and made plain only by observation of the practice of the artists who have excelled in that art. Criticism is but the hand-maid of creation; and the task of the commentator is impossible when he lacks material for comment. Then is he reduced to the needless and profitless exercise of inventing Rules for an art which he has not been able to observe in the actual process. Whenever the dramatic critic has toiled vainly because there was no living drama in his own tongue and in his own time to inspire him and to guide him, he has been led unfailingly to deal with the drama as tho it were solely a department of literature, to be weighed on literary scales only and to be measured merely by literary standards.

Even when the theater is active and productive, it is difficult enough for the critic to remember always that the drama does not lie wholly within the limits of literature. No doubt, it is mainly by its literary qualities that a drama survives, by its invention, by its structure, by its style, by its veracity of character, by its ethical integrity; but it is by its non-literary qualities that it has been able at first to succeed on the stage, by its theatrical effectiveness, its histrionic opportunities, its picturesqueness when performed.

In the long, interesting and instructive history of dramatic criticism—a history which has not

yet tempted to its telling any scholar equipt with
a wide acquaintance with literature and a deep
understanding of the theater—in this long history
two names stand out preëminent, the names of
Aristotle and of Lessing. The names of the
Alexandrian writers are forgotten; and the names
of the critics of the Italian Renascence are familiar
only to devoted specialists. It may be admitted that the names of Sidney and of Boileau
are still cherisht; but the code they declared has
long been discredited and disestablisht. The
names of Gottsched and of La Harpe carry no
weight in the twentieth century, even to those
who chance to remember that once they were
loudly acclaimed as arbiters of taste. Many a
name that for a season blazed brilliantly in the
sky is as disregarded today as the stick of a burnt-
out rocket. Who pays any attention today to
Schlegel, sunk beneath the wave of oblivion because of the rancor of his political prejudices and
because of the frequent falsity of his general ideas?
Who knows now, or cares to know, that a century ago Népomucène Lemercier catalogued the
twenty-five rules which tragedy must obey and the
twenty-two rules to which comedy must conform?
Critics of the drama come and go; they rise and
fall; they have their little fame, and sometimes
they may survive to see it fade away. Reputation is as fleeting in criticism as it is in creation;
and the promulgators of dramatic doctrine are

no more likely to retain popular esteem than the poets and the playwrights they have sought to guide and to govern. The winds of doctrine shift with the changing years, and often with startling suddenness. But however bitterly the veering breezes may blow, the names of Aristotle and of Lessing stand where they have stood these many years.

The pleasure that we find in the selection of the Hundred Best Books or of the Hundred Finest Pictures is futile; but there is always profit in striving to recognize with certainty the Best Poets and the Best Painters, be they a dozen or a score or a hundred. And when we seek to get a firm grasp upon the abiding principles of any art, it is no less profitable for us to ascertain who are the Best Critics of that art. In the analysis and interpretation of the art of the drama the supreme chiefs are Aristotle and Lessing, these two and no others. They are theorists, it is true, as were the Alexandrians and the Italians, whose vogue was evanescent; but their theories were solidly rooted in accurate observation of the acted drama. The laws they declared are as valid today as ever; their judgments have been confirmed in the supreme court over which Time presides; and even their *obiter dicta* are still significant.

When we seek to spy out the reasons why the solid authority of Aristotle and Lessing endures thru the ages, we must begin by crediting both of them with the fourfold qualifications without which all efforts at criticism are barren. They had insight and equipment, sympathy and dis-interestedness. They did not possess all of these qualifications in an equal degree; but all four of these they did possess not only sufficiently but abundantly. They had the innate gift of analysis; they had material for comparison; they had a natural relish for the best; and they sought al-ways to see the thing as it is, without bias, taking their personal prejudices out of the way. What-ever deduction may be indicated from this asser-tion must be directed to two points only; Aristotle may be held to be a little limited in his equip-ment by the fact that he had no other dramatic literature to compare with that of his country-men; and Lessing may be thought to be more than a little limited in his disinterestedness by his desire to discredit and to destroy the influence of the French classicists.

Then the ultimate validity of their criticism is due partly to the fact that their vision was not circumscribed by the walls of the playhouse; they toiled in other fields and they knew many things wholly unrelated to the theater. Their reputations do not rest solely, or even chiefly, on their work as expounders of dramaturgic doctrine. One might go so far as to say that altho Aristotle and Lessing are the supreme dramatic critics, their fame would scarcely be less if they had never written a word about the theater. No man can know his own subject thoroly if his own subject is all that he knows; he needs to wander afield and to be interested in many other things if he is to attain breadth of survey even in his own specialty. Aristotle, and Lessing also, had that cognate culture, without which, as Mr. Brownell has insisted, "specific erudition produces a rather lean result."

But altho their vision was not contracted within the limits of the theater, it is always in the theater itself that they conceive themselves to be sitting when they come to the criticism of a play. They are never mere readers of literature but always spectators of the acted drama. They are ever thinking in terms of the theater itself. "A play has this peculiarity and distinction," said Brunetière, "that being written to be acted, it is not complete in itself and it cannot be detacht from the material conditions of scenic representation and from the nature of the public for which it is destined." Aristotle and Lessing kept in mind the nature of the public to which the playwrights they were discussing had appealed; and they never overlookt the material conditions of scenic representation. By a constant effort of imaginative sympathy they were able to transport themselves in fancy from the desk where they sat alone to a seat in front of the actors and by

65

the side of a crowd of other spectators. It is by their understanding of the Siamese-twinship of the drama and the theater that their theories are validated.

The principles they establisht for dramatic literature were derived from the practice of successful playwrights. These principles had nothing etherial or volatile; they were rooted in common sense. What Professor Giddings says about Aristotle as an interpreter of the science of government is equally true about Aristotle as an expounder of the art of poetry: "Aristotle was indeed one of the greatest of theorists; but he is likewise one of the shrewdest judges of what we call practical politics"; and "his theories grew out of his observations, and they formulate vital principles from concrete social conditions." And Lessing was scarcely less shrewd than Aristotle as a judge of practical playmaking, having even the advantage of being himself a successful playwright, practising what he preacht.

In other words, the dramatic criticism of Aristotle and Lessing is expert criticism; and it is highly technical. As the technical principles of every art endure thru the ages unchanged, however much its devices may be modified by altered conditions, the precepts proposed by Aristotle and by Lessing state permanent and essential principles of dramaturgy. Indeed, it is the insistence of Aristotle upon sheer technic which has misled

so many of his commentators, who have accepted
him as an inspired lawgiver, coming down from
the mountain with the tables of stone in his hand,
instead of seeing that he is only presenting shrewd
deductions from his own observations in the
theater when the masterpieces of the Greek drama
were performed before his gaze.

II

IN its size, in its material conditions, in its spectators, the Globe theater in London was very
unlike the theater of Dionysus in Athens; the
picture-frame stage of our latter-day playhouse
is very unlike the platform-stage of the Elizabethans; but none the less are the essential principles which guided Shakspere in his greatest
tragedies, when his ambition was aroused and
when he was exerting all his powers, the same as
those which governed Sophocles and which
Aristotle declared,—as they are the same which
Molière followed in his turn and which Ibsen was
to obey in our own time. These essential principles are independent of the changes in the size
and material conditions of the various theaters
that have succeeded one another in the past
twenty-five centuries. It is because Aristotle was
able to lay hold of the most important of these
principles more than two thousand years ago
that he remains constantly up-to-date, with no

danger of ever falling out-of-date. This is the reason why his name is now constantly invoked by the more important reviewers of the contemporary drama, while the names of Johnson and Pope, of Boileau and Horace are allowed to languish in innocuous desuetude.

This modernness of Aristotle's dramatic theories is due mainly to his modesty in not assuming the attitude of the inspired lawgiver. He was never arrogant, as Schlegel was. He contented himself with pointing out the principles which seemed to him to underly the practices of the dramatic poets of accredited supremacy. He suggested that if Sophocles apparently obeys certain rules, why, then it might be well if all those who may be ambitious to compose plays should also obey these rules. He conceived himself as giving counsel, and as advising 'prentice playwrights how best they could model themselves on the masters. His conclusions were tentative, as becomes a man of science, conscious that the results of any inquiry are never final.

It need not surprize us that the uneasy Italian commentators of Aristotle did not see him in this light, that they ascribed to him their own dictatorial attitude. They knew Seneca better than they knew Sophocles; and they really relisht the declamatory rhetoric of the Hispano-Roman more than the austere poetry and the masterly plotting of the great Greek. They knew Horace better than they knew Aristotle—Horace, who in all his life may never have seen a good play well acted, and whose precepts are detacht from practize, being borrowed second-hand from the Alexandrian criticasters of the Hellenistic decadence. Perhaps it is not too much to say that the supersubtle Italians read Aristotle thru the spectacles of Horace; and because Horace spoke as one having authority, they believed that Aristotle also was a promulgator of implacable decrees. When they failed to find in his text a code as complete or as rigid as they desired, in their intolerance they did not hesitate to draft new laws in the name of Aristotle. They sanctified the elaborate classicist doctrine of the drama by sheltering it under his revered authority. It is no wonder that when the romanticist revolt came, as it had to come, some of its leaders should have sneered at Aristotle, holding him responsible for the perverted theories put forth by his insatiable commentators. Nor is there any wonder that Aristotle should have come into his own again, after the "magniloquent silhouettes of romanticist drama,"—as Mr. Huneker has called them—shrivelled from the stage.

Aristotle's discussion of playmaking is incidental to his larger discussion of poetry. It has come down to us incomplete and fragmentary. We cannot be assured that we have his own text. We are in doubt whether what we now possess is only a portion of a careful treatise made ready for publication by Aristotle, or whether it is only a collection of memorandums set down loosely to aid him in lecturing. There are even commentators who hold that our manuscripts are due not to Aristotle himself but to some ardent disciple who took notes to preserve as best he could the utterances of the master. The late Jules Lemaitre was of the second of these opinions, finding confirmation for it in the famous sentence about the tragic "purgation" of passion. "No doubt Aristotle jotted this down as a simple memorandum,—for it is incomplete and badly constructed, containing a figure of speech both bizarre and ill-prepared; and it is very like those notes, intelligible only to ourselves which we set down in a notebook with telegraphic or hieroglyphic brevity."

In the same criticism,—an account of Corneille's vain efforts to reconcile his own practice with the precepts of Aristotle,—Lemaitre dwelt on the patent absurdity of supposing that all the precepts of Aristotle are final for all time and in all countries, since the Greek philosopher was making remarks only about the tragedies of his own day,—"that is to say, about operas of a kind, which were acted and sung two or three times a year at great festivals," and of which Aristotle "might have seen or read a hundred at most, for they were not very numerous," probably outlining "his theories from his study of a score of prize-winning plays."

It is not to be wondered at that a few of Aristotle's remarks are applicable only to Greek tragedies,—"operas of a kind";—what is wonderful is that so many of them are acceptable when applied to modern plays wholly unlike Greek tragedies, and that a critic as acute as Emile Faguet was not guilty of wilful paradox when he asserted that the more he studied the 'Poetics' the more assured he felt that Aristotle "has given us rather the theory of French tragedy than that of Greek tragedy."

What are the principles of playmaking declared by Aristotle and as dominant today as they were in his own time? First of all, there is a clear recognition of the essential relation of the drama to the theater, with its declamation, its gestures, its spectacle, and above all, with its spectators whom the playwright has to interest, to arouse, and to hold.

Secondly, there is an equally clear recognition of the supreme importance of the action, the story, the plot;—"most important of all is the structure of the incidents, for a play is an imitation, not of men, but of an action and of life,— of happiness and misery; and happiness and misery consist in action, the end of human life being a mode of action, not a quality. . . . Dramatic action, therefore, is not with a view to

71

the representation of character; character comes in as subsidiary to the action. Hence the incidents and the plot are the end of a tragedy; and the end is the chief thing of all. Again, without action there cannot be a tragedy; there may be without character. . . . The poet should be a maker of plots rather than of verses; since he is a poet because he imitates, and what he imitates are actions."

This is a hard saying for the defenders of the closet-drama, for it implies that merely as a play the 'Two Orphans' is superior to the 'Blot in the 'Scutcheon,' yet this would be denied by no competent dramatic critic. Jules Lemaitre called attention to the accuracy of Aristotle's clear distinctions and pointed out that modern melodrama makes use of general types, often traditional and empty of veracity; and that plays with no atom of observation or of truth may move us on the stage by virtue of their situations alone, of their emotional appeal. "The object of the theater is to represent a man *acting*, and therefore to exhibit him to us not as he is himself, but as he bears himself in his relations with other men and under the influence of accidental circumstances. Now, if the playwright is also an observer and a psychologist, if he is capable of letting us pierce to the core of a character, of an original soul, in the brief moment when this soul is reacting against an external accident, evidently the result will be more valuable. Yet altho this merit is a welcome addition, it is not indispensable in the theater. In short, the drama interests us, not predominantly by the depicting of human nature, but primarily by situations and only secondarily by the feelings of those therein involved."

Thirdly, a play must have unity of purpose. "Tragedy is an imitation of an action that is complete and whole and of a certain magnitude. . . . A whole is that which has a beginning, a middle and an end. . . . A well constructed plot, therefore, must neither begin nor end at haphazard. . . . Of all plots and actions the episodic are the worst; I call a plot *episodic* in which the episodes or acts succeed one another without probable or necessary sequence."

Fourthly, the story of a play must be plausible. "It is not the function of the poet to relate what has happened but what may happen,—what is possible according to the law of probability or necessity."

Fifthly, the playwright must never forget the playhouse and must always seek to foresee the effect to be produced when his play is actually performed. "In constructing the plot and working it out with the help of language, the poet should place the scene, as far as possible, before his eyes. In this way, seeing everything with the utmost vividness, as if he were a spectator of the action, he will discover what is in keeping with it and will be most unlikely to overlook inconsistencies."

Sixthly, the tragic poet must avoid both the commonplace and the magniloquent:—"The perfection of style is to be clear without being mean."

Here are a few of the most significant of Aristotle's suggestions to intending dramatists; they are simple enough all of them, and obvious enough, not to say indisputable. Yet they are sufficient to justify the assertion of Professor Bywater that when Aristotle was engaged only in showing how to construct a play in accord with the material conditions of the Athenian theater, he succeeded also "in formulating once for all the great first principles of dramatic art, the canons of dramatic logic, which even the most adventurous of modern dramatists can only at his peril forget or set at naught."

III

THE modern appreciation of Aristotle dates from Lessing, for it was the German critic who brusht aside the swarm of commentators to scrutinize the actual text of Aristotle and to see for himself what the Greek had actually said and what he actually meant. Lessing it was who made the pregnant suggestion that if we seek a full understanding of the 'Poetics' we must consider that truncated treatise in connection with Aristotle's better preserved 'Rhetoric' and

'Ethics.' We may hail Lessing, even tho he was greatly stimulated by Dacier and by Diderot, as the real leader of the movement to repeal the classicist code of the drama, erected mainly upon misunderstanding and misinterpretation of Aristotle.

Perhaps Lessing suffers today from the complete success of his polemic against the French critics who had adopted the windspun and wiredrawn theories of the Italians. In his day and in his country, it was generally believed that French tragedy was a revival of Greek tragedy and possibly even an improvement upon it. Nowadays we see so clearly that there was no basis for this belief that we find it difficult to understand how anybody could ever have held it; and therefore we are inclined to wonder why Lessing was so persistent in his demonstration of its absurdity. This is the inevitable disadvantage of all triumphant polemic, for when the victory is once won we fail to perceive the necessity for killing the dead over and over again.

Lessing was never overawed by the authority of Aristotle; but he insisted, first of all, on being shown the Greek's own words. He permitted no predecessor to hold him in pupillage, preferring to do his own thinking in his own fashion. He denied the jurisdiction of the French and the Italian and the Latin critics, tamely accepted by his contemporaries in Germany. He took nothing for granted; and he insisted on going back to first principles. He analized the judgments of those who have gone before; and he accepted their verdicts only when he himself found the decision in accord with the facts.

French criticism of the acted drama from the Abbé d'Aubignac to Népomucène Lemercier is not so foolish as those who have never read it may be inclined to suppose. The classicist code is hard and narrow, and it imposes upon its interpreters not a few absurdities; but these interpreters make shrewd suggestions here and there. Marmontel's advice to aspiring playwrights is rich in sensible remarks; but where Marmontel only scratcht the surface, Lessing cut to the core. Lemercier's twenty-five rules for tragedy and his twenty-two rules for comedy, altho pedantically promulgated, are most of them acceptable enough; but Lessing did not descend to externalities like these, being moved always to ascertain the inner qualities which alone vitalize a work of art. Diderot, from whom Lessing borrowed a great deal—combating French influence with arms captured from a Frenchman—was fertile in suggestive ideas, but he was rarely trustworthy; and the author of the 'Laocoön' was ever a sounder critic of art than the author of the 'Paradox on the Comedian.' The German never let himself be led astray by his own theories, and he achieved a consistency denied to the gifted but irregular Frenchman, partly because his equipment was

76

more solid and partly because his insight was more penetrating.

Mézières, in his preface to the French translation of the 'Hamburg Dramaturgy,' had no difficulty in showing the extent of Lessing's indebtedness to Diderot and also in exhibiting Lessing's occasionally eratic opinions. Mézières pointed out that Lessing allowed himself the astounding liberty of calling the comedy of Destouches finer than the comedy of Molière, and of vaunting his own ability to rehandle the themes of Corneille and Racine more effectively than they had done. It is true that Lessing was not only a critic of the drama but also a creator of it, and that his own pieces are the earliest of German plays to establish themselves in the theater and to keep the stage after a century and a half. But this does not justify his airy assertion that he could surpass Corneille and Racine in their own field.

The explanation of his uncharacteristic boast is to be found in the fact that Lessing was fighting Voltaire, and that he was thus tempted to disparage Corneille and Racine, in whose footsteps Voltaire was following. The German critic-creator wisht to explode the belief of his countrymen in the infallibility of French criticism and in the indisputable superiority of French tragedy. In the ardor of battle he was not always so particular as he might be in the choice of weapons he snatcht up for attack and defense. As Lowell pointed out, Lessing's intellect "was commonly stirred to motion by the impulse of other minds, and struck out its brightest flashes by collision with them." It must be remembered also that Lessing's discussion of dramatic art is not a treatise like Aristotle's, written out at leisure after full premeditation; it is a journalistic job, composed as occasion served; its successive chapters, if they may be so called, are evoked by the particular plays which chanced to be produced at the Hamburg theater. Very few of these plays are known today, even by name, except to readers of the 'Dramaturgy.' It is testimony to Lessing's critical faculty that he could find a suggestive text for shrewd comment in pretentious German pieces and in artless German adaptations from contemporary French drama. As subject matter for discussion, Lessing lackt precisely what Aristotle had,—a living dramatic literature in his own language. Nor had he been privileged to behold on the stage any of the masterpieces of Shakspere and Calderon with which he had acquainted himself in the study. Where Aristotle had a body of doctrine clearly and completely thought out before he began on his book, Lessing had to extemporize his opinions from day to day during his single year of service as theatrical reviewer. There need be no wonder that the 'Hamburg Dramaturgy' is not compact; and the real cause for surprize is that the collected articles are as coherent and as consistent as they are. Nor is there any necessity to deny that some of these articles reveal themselves now as mere journalism, sufficient unto the day but lacking in permanence, or that Lessing does not hesitate now and again to avail himself of the privileges of the journalist,—to reiterate, to exaggerate even if need be, to emphasize his assertions by overstatement so as to force his casual readers to apprehend his meaning. That there are dry places here and there is due to the aridity of the plays he had perforce to deal with. This was unfortunate for Lessing, who seems to have wearied of his hortatory task before the year of his servitude was out; and it was also unfortunate for us since the finer the work of art to be criticized the more strenuous is likely to be the effort of the critic to appreciate it worthily.

Even if the year's work which makes up the 'Hamburg Dramaturgy' must be described as journalism, still bearing the traces of its newspaper origin, we cannot but recognize in Lessing an incomparable journalist, without peer in insight and in equipment, abundant in sympathy for what is best,—altho a little lacking in disinterestedness so far as the French are concerned. And for journalism his style was exactly adapted. He was so clear, so sharp-sighted, so plain-spoken, so sturdy in common sense that he frequently appeared to be witty, altho his wit was rarely verbal or merely wit for its own sake. It never had the flashing felicity of Voltaire's style—of that Voltaire whom Lessing admired even while attacking. It was from Voltaire that Lessing borrowed the useful device of using narrative as an implicit criticism of the plot under consideration. And we may apply to Lessing the praise Lord Morley bestowed on Voltaire, that his "work, from first to last, was alert with unquenchable life. Some of it, much of it, has ceased to be alive for us now. . . . Yet we recognize that none of it was ever the dreary still-birth of a mind of hearsays. There is no mechanical transmission of untested bits of current coin."

Yet few of Lessing's precepts of playmaking, rooted as they are in common sense and instantly acceptable by all students of the stage, can be detacht from the criticism of the specific pieces that evoked them. He restated principles laid down by Aristotle; he clarified pregnant sayings of Diderot; he may have derived from d'Aubignac the belief that unflinching fidelity to the accidental facts of history is not to be demanded from the writer of a historical play,—altho he may have found this implicit in one of Aristotle's paragraphs. He was forever going back to the great Greek and he was incessant in declaring that, after all, Aristotle was not a Frenchman.

He was quite as insistent in tackling Voltaire and in asserting that after all the great Frenchman was not a Greek. He spent half-a-hundred pages to prove that Voltaire had taken his 'Mérope' from Maffei and had failed to better it in the borrowing. And he was sometimes more negative than affirmative, more anxious to discredit the French critics and to disestablish the classicist theorists than to declare his own sounder and saner principles.

IV

ARISTOTLE and Lessing are the two foremost theorists of the theater; and there is no third to be rankt with them. Yet at an interval after them and far in advance of any fourth claimant, comes Francisque Sarcey, inferior to both in insight and equipment, even if not inferior in sympathy and disinterestedness. He was a journalist like Lessing; but he did not confine his activity to a single year, continuing it in fact for nearly two score years. He resembled Lessing again in that he did not begin with a body of doctrine, with a code of laws formulated in advance of any possible application. Like the English judges he develop the law slowly from the successive cases that were brought before him, until at the last he arrived at a consciousness of the fundamental principles of the art he loved devotedly his whole life long.

Sarcey's body of doctrine, when once he was in possession of it, was his own; it was the result of his incomparable experience of the theater and of his incessant study of the spectators. As a consequence of his integrity and of his critical shrewdness, his doctrine is substantially identical with Aristotle's and with Lessing's. Independently he arrived at the same conclusions that they had reacht before him. As he told me once, whenever he took down the French translation of the 'Hamburg Dramaturgy' and found that Lessing had anticipated him in one of his own discoveries, he rejoiced, feeling thereby reinforced in his conviction that his discovery was solidly based on truth.

Sarcey was more narrowly a man of the theater than either Aristotle or Lessing; and this is perhaps a main reason why he does not deserve to be placed by their side. It is true that he had many outside interests and that he was an indefatigable writer on all sorts of topics, literary and social and political; but his heart was ever in the theater, and to him the art of the drama had a supreme importance which it had not to Lessing or to Aristotle, because they had a broader outlook than he, a more comprehensive philosophy.

Yet whatever his limitations, he was the most inspiring and suggestive critic of the acted drama in the nineteenth century. Not so dogmatic as Brunetière, not so brilliant as Lemaitre, not

so versatile as Faguet, he easily surpast
all three in his intimacy with the playhouse and
with its people, actors as well as authors; and he
was therefore a sounder critic of that part of the
drama which is more specifically of the theater.
His experience was far longer than Lessing's and
his subject matter is richer and more varied.
Where Aristotle had the Greek drama as his sole
material for the deduction of his principles and
where Lessing had only the plays which happened
to be acted in a single German theater in a single
year, even tho he ranged at will in search of
parallels thruout dramatic literature, Sarcey had
all the theaters of the capital of France for forty
years when they were representing not only the
contemporary and the classic drama in his own
tongue but also many of the masterpieces of the
drama in other literatures, ancient and modern.

It may be admitted that Sarcey did not profit
as he might by his opportunity to see on the stage
the mightiest plays of Greece and England. He
was too fundamentally a man of his own country, and even of his own time, really to relish
Sophocles and Shakspere. Moreover, he was a
little inclined to be the slave of his own doctrine
and to hold this a little too narrowly. He was
only following the wise Aristotle and the shrewd
Lessing when he insisted on the superior importance of plot, of story, of action; but he went
ahead of them in his appreciation of the mechan-

ical dexterity of plotmaking. In fact, he was inclined almost to accept skill in craftsmanship, the skill of a Scribe, for example, as the final word in dramatic accomplishment, instead of seeing clearly that this skill is only the first word. Construction, the adroit building up of a series of situations—this is a prime requisite of dramatic art, without which the art cannot exist; but it is only the beginning and it can never be an end in itself, as it was in the so-called "well-made play" of Scribe and of the cloud of collaborators and disciples that encompast Scribe about.

Still it must be urged that in insisting upon the duty of providing every play with an inner skeleton strong enough to support it unaided, even if he insisted at times a little too exclusively upon this, Sarcey was exerting a most wholesome influence, especially in these days when the novelists are invading the theater and when some of them seek to confuse the essential differences between the art of the drama and the art of prose-fiction. The first and foremost of these differences is due to the immitigable fact that the novel may appeal only to the individual reader whereas the play must appeal to a crowd of spectators. The theater is "a function of the crowd," so a British critic has declared; and in so declaring he was only echoing Sarcey, who asserted that he could deduce all the laws of dramatic art from the single fact that every play implies the presence of an

audience. This is why Sarcey was so indefatigable in his observation of the playgoers and in his
analysis of their characteristics, their predilec-
tions, their prejudices, their unconscious preferences. Here he was doing explicitly what Aristotle
and Lessing had done implicitly.

Sarcey's attitude when he set himself down at
the first performance of a new play was very like
that of the burgher of Paris who ventured to take
a hand in the exacerbated discussion evoked by
Corneille's 'Cid.' "I have never read Aristotle
and I know nothing about the Rules, but I
decide upon the merit of a play in proportion to
the pleasure I receive." Sarcey had read Aristotle and he was familiar with the Rules; but he
judged tragedy and comedy, problem-play and
farce, in proportion to the pleasure he himself
received, but also and more particularly in proportion to the pleasure received by his fellow spectators. He came in time to be very expert in
interpreting these unconscious preferences of the
crowd, which the dramatist has always to reckon
with.

His suggestive theory of the scenes inherent in every story, which demand to be shown
in action, the famous theory of the *scènes à faire*,
Obligatory Scenes, was the result of his ability
to translate the dumb disappointment of the
playgoers when the dramatist neglects to set before their eyes the interesting episode he has led

85

them to expect. This is one of Sarcey's most important contributions to the theory of the theater; and it is his own, altho there are intimations of it in earlier writers—notably in Corneille's third 'Discourse on the Dramatic Poem.' Sarcey may have had predecessors also in his theory of the necessary conventions of the drama. Every art can exist only by its departure from the facts of life; the painter and the sculptor, for example, are permitted to represent men as motionless, altho absolute absence of movement is impossible to human beings. The drama demands the condensation and heightening of the dialog and the suppression of everything accidental, altho accident surrounds us on all sides. These liberties with life are for the benefit of the spectators in the theater, who want to see and to hear and have their interest focust upon the essentials of the story set before them on the stage; and by convention, that is by tacit agreement, by implied contract, the spectators gladly permit the playwright to depart from the facts of life so that he can delight them with the truth of life.

It is greatly to be regretted that Sarcey never composed his promised 'History of Dramatic Conventions'; but as he once said to me, "If I had ever written my book, with what could I fill my weekly articles?" Here he spoke out in accord with his frank and sturdy common sense— that common sense which according to Vauvenargues must be credited rather to character than to intellect.

The influence of Lessing on the contemporary German theater was due not so much to his dramatic criticism as to his dramatic creation,—to the three or four plays in which he proved that it was possible to put German life and German character on the stage at once effectively and sincerely. Sarcey may have written a trifling farce or two in his youth, but his influence on the contemporary French theater was due wholly to his criticism. He had the good fortune, denied to Lessing, of working in a period when there was a living dramatic literature in his own language. He was able to interpret and to encourage Augier and Dumas fils, Meilhac and Halévy, Labiche and Rostand, very much as Boileau had interpreted and encouraged Molière. The principles of playmaking these dramatists were applying were precisely those which Sarcey was proclaiming.

It is difficult to overestimate the influence exerted by Sarcey upon the development of the drama in France in the final third of the nineteenth century. His theories of the theater were adopted and disseminated by other critics, often by writers as different as Brunetière, Lemaitre and Faguet. In the main, and for years, this influence was helpful; yet a time came at last when Sarcey's principles, as he himself continued to declare them, were felt to be a little too narrow and a little too rigidly insisted upon. M. Gustave Lanson, for example, has denounced Sarcey for unduly confining his attention to technic, for overvaluing the form of a play at the expense of its content, and for following rather than guiding the taste of the public. There is a certain justice in these charges; and it may be admitted that in his old age Sarcey was a willing prisoner in his own code of the drama. But to grant this is not to deny the abiding utility of his contributions to the theory of the theater.

V

At bottom the body of doctrine which Sarcey built up for his own use as a critic of the acted drama is substantially the same as that which we find in Lessing and in Aristotle. These three theorists of the theater estimate plays primarily by the test of the playhouse and by analysis of the desires of the playgoers. The several playhouses in which the Greek and the German and the Frenchman took their seats varied widely in their physical conditions, in their dimensions and in their shapes. But these various playhouses had one characteristic in common, a characteristic which is to be discovered in almost every kind of theater before the final quarter of the nineteenth century. In all these playhouses, the actor was surrounded on three sides by the audience.

88

In the Attic theater the performers stood in the orchestra which curved into the hillside of the Acropolis; in Shakspere's theater, as in Molière's, certain spectators were accommodated with seats on the stage itself; and in the theaters for which Beaumarchais and Sheridan composed their comedies the stage jutted out far into the house, so that the actors actually turned their backs on a certain proportion of the audience. But in the final quarter of the nineteenth century this platform-stage gave way to the picture-frame stage to which we are accustomed in our snug modern theaters; and nowadays the actor is not in close proximity to the spectators; he is not surrounded by them on three sides; he is withdrawn behind a picture-frame; and he is bidden not to get out of the picture.

This change from the platform-stage of the past to the picture-frame stage of the present is perhaps the most important which has ever taken place in all the long history of the drama; and it is too recent for us to forecast all its consequences, altho we may be certain that they will be many and striking, influencing the method of every writer for the stage. As the dramatist always plans his plays with the intent and the desire of seeing them performed before an audience, by actors, and in a theater, any change in the conditions of the theater will force changes in the method of both actors and dramatist, and it may also bring about changes in the unconscious preferences of the audience. It is an interesting question whether these changes will or will not invalidate in any way the accredited theory of the theater as this has been expounded by Lessing and Aristotle, who had no other plays as a basis of study than those composed in accord with the conditions of the platform-stage; and even Sarcey could see only the beginnings of the more modern drama composed specifically for the picture-frame stage.

The audiences of the past who knew only the platform-stage, expected to see thereon a story, with a well-knit plot, setting forth a clash of contending desires. Will the spectators of the future, sitting in front of the picture-frame stage, retain this expectation? Or will they be contented with pictures of life and character held together by a slacker thread of story, scarcely strong enough to be called a plot, and lacking in any clearly defined conflict of volition? More than twenty years ago, William Archer, that acutest of British dramatic critics, posed this question clearly: "What is the essential element of drama? Is it the telling of a story after a certain establisht method which has been found by long experience to answer to the mental requirements of an average audience? Or is it the mere scenic presentment of passages from real life? Should the dramatist look primarily to action, letting character take its chance? Or primarily to character, letting action look after itself?"

Mr. Archer exprest his own sympathy with the latter opinion, holding that it was supplanting the former, which he admitted to have been dominant for fifty years and which he identified with Sarcey. But he might have identified it with Aristotle and admitted that it had been dominant for two thousand years. Nothing could be clearer or more emphatic than the declaration earlier quoted from Aristotle that if you string together a set of speeches expressive of character, and well finisht in point of diction and thought, "you will not produce the essential dramatic effect nearly so well as with a play, which, however deficient in these aspects yet has a plot and artistically constructed incidents." To this Mr. Archer might answer that when Aristotle and Sarcey insisted on the superior value of plot over character in arousing and retaining the interest of the average audience, they could not foresee that the spectators of the future in front of a picture-frame stage might not have precisely the same unconscious preferences as the spectators of the past almost surrounding the platform-stage—especially after these spectators may have had their interest focust on character, rather than on story, by the works of the many realists who have trod the trail blazed by Balzac.

And to this retort, the rejoinder is easy,—indeed, Mr. Archer may despise it as a little too easy. Admitting that the change in the playhouse may bring about an unforeseen change in the attitude of the more highly cultivated playgoers, still it is a little unlikely that the theories of the theater which we find expounded by Aristotle first, then by Lessing, and lastly by Sarcey, will turn out to be any less valid in the next century than they have proved themselves to be in the past twenty centuries. This much at least I may venture to predict without assuming the robe of a prophet—an unbecoming costume which I shall not dare to don so long as I recall George Eliot's assertion, that "of all the forms of human error prophecy is the most gratuitous."

(1915.)

V

IF SHAKSPERE SHOULD COME BACK?[*]

INGENIOUS wits have often amused themselves by imagining the possible return of a departed genius that he might mingle for a few hours with men of the present generation; and they have humorously speculated upon his emotions when he found himself once again in the life he had left centuries earlier. They have wondered what he would think about this world of ours today, the same as his of long ago and yet not the same. What would he miss that he might have expected to find? What would he find that he could never have expected? As he had been a human being when he was in the flesh, it is a safe guess that he would be interested first of all in himself, in the fate of his reputation, in the opinion in which he is now held by us who know him only thru his writings. And it is sad to think that many a genius would be grievously disappointed at the shrinkage of his fame. If he had hoped to see his books still alive, passing from hand to hand,

* This paper was written especially for 'A Book of Homage to Shakspere.' (Oxford University Press, 1916.)

familiar on the lips as household words, he might be shockt to discover that they survived solely in the silent obscurity of a complete edition, elaborately annotated and preserved on an upper shelf for external use only. On the other hand, there would be a genius now and then who had died without any real recognition of his immortal gifts and who, on his imagined return to earth, would be delighted to discover that he now bulkt bigger than he had ever dared to dream.

It is in this second and scanty group that Shakspere would belong. So far as we can judge from the sparse records of his life and from his own writings, he was modest and unassuming, never vaunting himself, never boasting and probably never puffed up by the belief that he had any reason to boast. What he had done was all in the day's work, a satisfaction to him as a craftsman when he saw that he had turned out a good job, but a keener satisfaction to him as a man of affairs that he was thereby getting on and laying by against the day when he might retire to Stratford to live the life of an English gentleman. Probably no other genius could now revisit the earth who would be more completely or more honestly astonisht by the effulgence of his fame. To suppose that this would not be exquisitely gratifying to him would be to suggest that he was not human. Yet a chief component of his broad humanity was his sense of humor; as a man he did not take himself too seriously, and as a ghost he would certainly smile at the ultra-seriousness of his eulogists and interpreters. A natural curiosity might lead him to look over a volume or two in the huge library of Shaksperian criticism; but these things would not detain him long. Being modest and unassuming still, he would soon weary of protracted praise.

It may be that Shakspere would linger long enough over his critics and his commentators to note that they have belauded him abundantly and superabundantly as a poet, as a philosopher, as a psychologist and as a playwright. He might even be puzzled by this fourfold classification of his gifts, failing for the moment to perceive its precision. When he read praise of his poetry, he would naturally expect to see it supported by quotation from his two narrative poems or from his one sonnet-sequence. Quite possibly he might be somewhat annoyed to observe that these juvenile verses, cordially received on their original publication, were now casually beplastered with perfunctory epithets, while the sincerest and most searching commendation was bestowed on the style and on the spirit of the plays, in their own day unconsidered by literary critics and not recognized as having any claim to be esteemed as literature. Yet this commendation, pleasing even if unforeseen, would not go to his head, since Shakspere—if we may venture to deduce his own

views from the scattered evidence in his plays—
had no unduly exalted opinion of poets or of
poetry.

If he might be agreeably surprized by the praise
lavisht on him as a poet, he would be frankly
bewildered by the commendation bestowed on him
as a philosopher. He knew that he was not a
man of solid learning, and that his reading,
even if wide enough for his immediate purpose,
had never been deep. He might admit that he
had a certain insight into the affairs of men and
a certain understanding of the intricate inter-
relations of human motives. But he could never
have considered himself as an original thinker,
advancing the boundaries of knowledge or push-
ing speculation closer to the confines of the un-
knowable. All he had sought to do in the way
of philosophy was now and again to phrase afresh
as best he could one or another of the eternal commonplaces, which need to be minted anew for the
use of every oncoming generation. If a natural
curiosity should tempt Shakspere to turn over
a few pages of his critics to discover exactly what
there was in his writings to give him rank among
the philosophers, he would probably be more
puzzled than before, until his sense of humor
effected a speedy rescue.

Bewildered as Shakspere might be to see himself dissected as a philosopher, he would be startled
to discover himself described also as a psychologist. To him the word itself would be unknown

and devoid of meaning, strange in sound and abhorrent in appearance. Even after it had been translated to him with explanation that he deserved discussion as a psychologist because he had created a host of veracious characters and had carried them thru the climax of their careers with subtle self-revelation, he might still wonder at this undue regard for the persons in his plays, whom he had considered not so much vital characters as effective acting-parts devised by him to suit the several capacities of his fellow actors, Burbage and Arnim, Heming and Condell. It might be that these creatures of his invention were more than parts fitted to these actors; but none the less had they taken shape in his brain first of all as parts intended specifically for performance by specific tragedians and comedians.

Only when Shakspere read commendation of his skill as a playwright, pure and simple, as a maker of plays to be performed by actors in a theater and before an audience, so constructed as to reward the efforts of the performers and to arouse and sustain the interest of the spectators— only then would he fail to be surprized at his posthumous reputation. He could not be unaware that his plays, comic and tragic, or at least that the best of them, written in the middle of his career as a dramatist, were more adroitly put together than the pieces of any of his predecessors and contemporaries. He could not forget the pains he had taken to knit together the successive situations into a compelling plot, to provide his story with an articulated backbone of controlling motive, to stiffen the action with moments of tense suspense, to urge it forward to its inevitable and irresistible climax, to achieve effects of contrast, and to relieve the tragic strain with inter-mittent humor. And even if it might mean little or nothing to him that he was exalted to a place beside and above Sophocles, the master of ancient tragedy, and Molière, the master of modern comedy, he might well be gratified to be recognized at last as a most accomplisht craftsman, ever dexterous in solving the problems of dramaturgic technic.

These fanciful suggestions are based on the belief that Shakspere—like every other of the supreme artists of the world—"builded better than he knew"; and that this is a main reason why his work abides unendingly interesting to us three centuries after his death. He seems to have written, partly for self-expression, of course, but chiefly for the delight of his contemporaries, with no thought for our opinion fifteen score years later; and yet he wrought so firmly, so largely and so loftily that we may rightly read into his works a host of meanings which he did not consciously intend—and for which he can take the credit, none the less, because only he could have put them there.

(1916.)

SHAKSPERIAN STAGE-TRADITIONS *

I

IT is unreasonable to expect that a financier, an artist or an actor should be able to talk entertainingly or to write instructively about his work in life. Sufficient is it if he can do this work satisfactorily, by dint of native gift; and we have no right to demand that he should always be conscious of his processes. It is the business of the financier to make money useful —of the artist to paint pictures or to model statues, to design buildings or to lay out gardens, —of the actor to delight us by the impersonation of character involved in situation; and it is not necessary that any one of them should be a theorist of the art whereby he earns his living. Yet now and again artists appear who happen to possess the critical faculty as well as the creative; and whenever one thus doubly endowed is moved to discuss the practice of his calling and the princi-

* This paper was contributed to 'Shaksperian Studies' (Columbia University Press, 1916); and it was read at a meeting of the American Academy of Arts and Letters, on March 30th, 1916.

ples of his craft, the rest of us will do well to listen attentively on the likely chance of picking up suggestions from which we may profit. What Reynolds and Fromentin and La Farge said about painting has an abiding value; and so have the less elaborate considerations of acting for which we are indebted to Talma, to Coquelin and to Jefferson.

In 'Art and the Actor,' Coquelin's plea for a fuller recognition of the importance and dignity of the histrionic profession, we are told that "there are but few masterpieces of dramatic literature so perfect that the actor cannot find something to add to them, if so inclined." This assertion will seem boastful only to those belated expounders who still seem to think that Sophocles and Shakspere and Molière wrote their plays solely for us moderns to peruse and who appear to believe blindly that these plays, composed expressly for the stage, will yet render up their full content to a lonely reader in the study. The perusal of the text will put us in possession of all the words of the dramatic poet; but only by performance in the theater itself is the spirit of a true drama made manifest and only before an actual audience can we gage its appeal to the soul of the multitude. The more familiar an open-minded reader may be with the printed lines of a dramatic masterpiece, the more likely is he to be delightedly surprised by the richness of detail and the fresh revelation of meaning when at last he has the privilege of seeing the play performed; and this rich revelation is always more or less due to the inventive skill of the performers in elaborating the latent possibilities of the dialog, in short, to the "something added by the actor."

The devoted student who dwells remote from theaters, and who is thereby deprived of all opportunity to see Shakspere's comedies and tragedies on the stage itself, may worship the poet with unquestioning idolatry; but he is in no position to estimate the full power of the playwright. He does not suspect how much more varied and colored and moving these comedies and these tragedies are when their characters are sustained by flesh-and-blood performers, when the words take on a new magic by the modulated tones of the human voice, and when the action is illustrated and illuminated by the appropriate by-play of the actors. This by-play, which is often team-play, this stage-business, as it is called, has been devised by successive generations of ingenious performers, every generation retaining the best of the inventions of its predecessors and handing these along (augmented by its own contributions) to the generation that comes after. Today the stage-manager who undertakes to produce a play of Shakspere's has at his command an immense body of these traditions, many of which he may prefer not to utilize, altho he is certain to preserve others which serve to bring into high relief the inner significance of vital episodes.

Such a body of gestures and actions is cherisht by the Comédie Française and utilized in its performances of Molière's comedies. "There are certain traditions at the Théâtre Français," so Coquelin told us in his address on the actor's art, "without which Molière is never played, and which the spectator, becoming a reader, mentally supplies as he sits by his fireside, as one supplies omissions in an incomplete copy." Some of these traditions are possibly derived directly from the original performances when the author-actor was the manager of the company; and some of them are the contribution of comedians as recent as Coquelin himself. They are so many, and they aid so amply in the interpretation of the plays, that Regnier brought out an edition of 'Tartuffe' wherein the best of the traditions which cluster around Molière's masterpiece were all carefully and elaborately set down to vivify the dialog. Regnier called this the 'Tartuffe des Comédiens'; and Coquelin once told me that he proposed to continue his teacher's task and to edit other of Molière's more important comedies with a similar amplitude of histrionic annotation. It is greatly to be regretted that the project was never carried out; no existing edition of Molière would surpass this in interest or in utility, if it had been prepared with the skill, the tact, and the scholarship displayed by Regnier in his single volume.

Coquelin asserted that the spectator of Molière, becoming a reader, supplied mentally the illustrative actions which he could not find in the text. But how about the reader of Molière who has never been a spectator? His memory cannot supply this material; and even if his imagination is active, he can never invent as adroitly or as abundantly as the actors themselves, charged with the high responsibility of actual performance and trained to scrutinize the dialog assiduously in search of histrionic opportunity. The task which Regnier began and which Coquelin failed to carry out, may yet be completed by one or another of the comedians of the Théâtre Français; and even before it is finally accomplisht for Molière, it may be undertaken for Shakspere. The Shaksperian traditions are as many, as varied and as helpful; and they are now kept alive only by word of mouth, descending orally from actor to actor or preserved by the industry of a chance stage-manager in the flagrant insecurity of an unprinted prompt-copy.

When Macready retired from the active practice of his profession, George Henry Lewes exprest the hope that the actor would devote his honorable leisure to the preparation of an edition of Shakspere, in which there should be due recognition of the fact that Shakspere was as great

as a playwright as he was as a poet. The actor
did not accept the invitation of the critic; and
even if he had, we may doubt whether he would
have condescended to record all the many traditions of the theater, some of which he himself devised, while others he inherited from John Kemble and Edmund Kean, to pass along to Edwin
Booth and Henry Irving. Sometimes a contemporary criticism has recorded for us the name
of the actor whose ingenuity was responsible for
a striking effect developt out of the unadorned
dialog and yet not discovered by any of his predecessors in the part; and sometimes the customary
business is so old that its origin must be ascribed
to a time whereof the memory of man runneth
not to the contrary.

While it is always interesting to know the name
of the performer who first enricht the text with
a felicitous accompaniment of pause and emphasis, glance and gesture, what is really important to remember is that there is no single scene
in any one of the more frequently acted comedies
and tragedies which has not thus been made more
pictorial and thereby more dramatic in the eyes
of the actual spectators. Every edition pre-
serves for us the words uttered by Othello and
Iago in the marvelously built up crescendo when
Iago distills the poison of jealousy drop by drop
until Othello writhes in his overwhelming agony.
But how did Iago deliver his corroding insinua-

tions? How did Othello listen to them? Were they standing or sitting? What was the arrangement of the room? How was the mounting action intensified by looks and movements? How did the two actors play into each other's hands to achieve the ultimate peak and summit to which all that went before had tended irresistibly? These things we do not find in any existing edition.

It is idle to say that these things are relatively unimportant and that we have Shakspere's words, which ought to suffice. Shakspere wrote his words specifically for actors, and for the interpretation and embellishment which only actors can give; and his words demand this interpretation and embellishment before they surrender their full content or disclose their ultimate potency. No commentary on Hamlet, of all the countless hundreds that have been written, would be a more useful aid to a larger understanding of his character than a detailed record of the readings, the gestures, the business employed in the successive performances of the part by Burbage and by Betterton, by Garrick and by Kemble, by Macready and by Forrest, by Booth and by Irving. It is not that any one of these renowned actors is necessarily superior in critical acumen to the more intellectual of the commentators; it is that they have been compelled by their professional training to acquire an insight into this character composed specifically for their use—an insight to be attained only in the theater itself and hopelessly unattainable in the library even by the most scholarly or by the most brilliant expositor.

II

OUTSIDE of her profession Mrs. Siddons was only an ordinary mortal; and the essay which she wrote on the character of Lady Macbeth is quite negligible. But inside of her profession she was a genius, gifted with an interpreting imagination by means of which she projected a more commanding and more sinister figure than had ever been suspected to be latent in the relatively few speeches of the comparatively brief part of Lady Macbeth. Mrs. Siddons created the character anew; she made it more dominating than it had ever been before; and in so doing she seems to have carried Shakspere's intentions to a point which he could not have foreseen. When we survey the tragedy as a whole, we perceive that the dramatist spent his main effort on Macbeth himself, on the hero-villain who begins and ends the play, and that the heroine-villain is only an accessory character, marvelously significant, no doubt, but nevertheless subordinate. In writing the words of Macbeth, so Fleming Jenkin finely suggested, Shakspere "cannot have had present to his mind all the gestures and expressions of Lady Macbeth as she listened," and yet this by-play of Mrs. Siddons "was such that the audience, looking at her, forgot to listen to Macbeth." What Shakspere supplied was a mightily etcht outline for the performer of the part to color superbly; and Shakspere is a masterly playwright partly because his plays ever abound in opportunities to be improved by the insight of inspired actors.

Fleeming Jenkin was not relying solely upon the casual discussion of Mrs. Siddons' acting preserved in contemporary criticisms; he was supported by the detailed record of her readings, her intonations, her pauses, her glances, her gestures and her movements made by a competent observer, Professor G. J. Bell, who annotated the text as he followed her performances night after night. And Professor Bell added to this invaluable account of what the great actress did in this great part, a summary of the total impression made by her in the tragedy:—"Of Lady Macbeth there is not a great deal in the play, but the wonderful genius of Mrs. Siddons makes it the whole. . . . Her turbulent and inhuman strength of spirit does all. She turns Macbeth to her purpose, makes him her mere instrument, guides, directs and inspires the whole plot. Like Macbeth's evil genius she hurries him on in the mad career of ambition and cruelty from which his nature would have shrunk." Possibly Shakspere meant this; certainly he supplied the material for it; but it was the actress who brought out all the hidden possibilities of the character to an extent that the poet could scarcely have anticipated.

Professor Bell declared that when she was impersonating Lady Macbeth, Mrs. Siddons was "not before an audience; her mind wrought up in high conception of her part, her eye never wandering, never for a moment idle, passion and sentiment continually betraying themselves. Her words are the accompaniments of her thoughts, scarcely necessary, you would imagine, to the expression, but highly raising it, and giving the full force of poetical effect."

This record of Mrs. Siddons' Lady Macbeth is testimony to the truth of one striking passage in the illuminating paper which Fleeming Jenkin prepared to accompany it. The words uttered by any one of Shakspere's chief characters, so the critic asserted, "do not by themselves supply the actor with one-hundredth part of the actions he has to perform. Every single word has to be spoken with just intonation and emphasis, while not a single intonation or emphasis is indicated by the printed copy. The actor must find the expression of face, the attitude of body, the action of the limbs, the pauses, the hurries—the life, in fact. There is no logical process by which all these things can be evolved out of the mere words of a part. The actor must go direct to nature and his own heart for the tones and the action by which he is to move his audience; these his author cannot give him, and in creating these, if he be a great actor, his art is supremely great." Here Fleeming Jenkin is putting into other words the almost contemporary assertion of Coquelin that "there are but few masterpieces so perfect that the actor cannot find something to add to them." And all that the supremely great actors can imagine to move an audience, the printed dialog is devoid of; and the mere reader in the library cannot restore it unless he has earlier been a spectator in the theater itself.

III

Just as Regnier's 'Tartuffe des Comédiens' afforded a model for the editing of Molière, so we have in English at least one attempt to supply an edition of a Shaksperian play as it was interpreted by the genius of a great actor. This is E. T. Mason's record of Salvini's Othello, in which we find all that the fortunate spectators of that massive performance need when they become readers and when they endeavor to supply mentally the tones and the gestures with which the Italian actor illuminated the English tragedy. Mr. Mason gave us portraits of the actor costumed for the part; and he supplied descriptions and diagrams of all the stage-sets used by Salvini. He set down the tragedian's readings, his glances and his gestures, and his movements about the stage; and so complete is this record that a lonely student who had never been able to see Othello performed would get from it a fuller disclosure of the essential energy of the tragedy than he could possibly have had before.

It is true that the lonely student might have been aided in the effect to evoke in his mind's eye an imagined performance by a collection and a comparison of contemporary criticisms of actual performances by Edmund Kean, by Macready and by Edwin Booth; and he would find especially helpful Lewes' noble tribute to Salvini's tremendous exhibition of power at the highest point of the wonderfully wrought scene in which Iago unchains the demon of jealousy in Othello. "But the whole house was swept along by the intense and finely graduated culmination of passion in the outburst, 'Villain, be sure you prove' when seizing Iago and shaking him as a lion might shake a wolf, he finishes by flinging him on the ground, raises his foot to trample on the wretch—and then a sudden revulsion of feeling checks the brutality of the act, the *gentleman* masters the *animal,* and with mingled remorse and disgust he stretches forth a hand to raise him up."

Yet eloquent as this passage is, it is not so

useful to the lonely student as Mr. Mason's mi-
nute account of all that was done in the course
of the entire act of which this was the climax.
Helpful also are the invaluable notes on his own
procedure when acting Othello or Iago contributed by Edwin Booth to the volume on 'Othello'
in Furness' 'Variorum Edition.'   More than any
preceding editor did Furness perceive the importance of considering the actors' specific contribution to an adequate understanding of Shakspere's merits as a playwright; and therefore all
the later volumes of the 'Variorum' are enricht
by more or less criticism of actual performances,
often with indication of readings and of business.
Here and there also in the ample volumes of William Winter's 'Shakspere on the Stage' we find
loving record of the manner in which culminating
moments were rendered by the foremost Shaksperian actors and actresses of the past half-cen-
tury.   For example, Winter has preserved for
us the interesting fact that it was Adelaide Neil-
son who first caused Juliet on the balcony to pluck
the flowers from her breast and to throw them
down to Romeo with an apparently unpremeditated gesture expressive of the ecstasy of her
overmastering passion.

Again in Clara Morris' account of her earlier years on the stage she credits herself with
the invention of an intensification of the dramatic effect in the final act of 'Othello.'   Al-

tho she was then only a slip of a girl she was called upon to impersonate the mature Emilia. After the death of Desdemona Emilia gives the alarm, crying aloud,

> Help! Help! Oh, help!
> The Moor hath killed my mistress! Murder! Murder!

and then the bell tolls a general alarm. The young actress arranged with the prompter that the bell should sound immediately after her shriek for

> Help! Help!

After this first stroke she raised her voice and cried,

> Help! Oh, help!

whereupon the bell rang out again and again. Instantly she resumed her outcry,

> The Moor hath killed my mistress!

And then the bell once more tolled the alarm. Finally she shriekt,

> Murder! Murder!

and the tolling was repeated until Montano and Gratiano and Iago rush in. Miss Morris is pleased to inform us that the result of this novel punctuation of her lines by the brazen tongue of the tocsin was to make her voice seem to combine with the clangor and to soar above it.

It would be pleasant to know whether or not the late William F. Owen should be credited with the devising of the felicitous business which enhanced Falstaff's reception of Prince Hal's exposure of his mendacity in the matter of the men in buckram, when a condensation of the two parts of 'Henry IV' was produced by Robert Taber and Julia Marlowe. After Falstaff has told his tale the Prince and Poins corner him. The scene represented the tavern at Eastcheap with its huge fireplace before which stood a spacious armchair with its back to the audience. After Falstaff had met the Prince's incredulity with abuse, he cried, "O for breath to utter!" and then he sank into the chair, sputtering out his final insults. Whereupon the Prince explained that:— "We two saw you four set upon four, and were masters of their wealth. Mark now, how plain a tale shall put you down."

As soon as Falstaff was convinced that his bluff was about to be called he shrank into the chair and the back of his head was no longer to be seen; so the Prince stated his case to an invisible Falstaff, ending with "What trick? what device? what starting hole cans't thou now find out, to hide thee from this open and apparent shame?" Then Henry paused for a reply and it was so long in coming, that Poins backed up the Prince, saying, "Come, let's hear, Jack. What trick hast thou now?"

Falstaff out of sight of the audience had twisted himself about in the chair until he was kneeling on it; and he slowly raised his face above its back—

a face wreathed with smiles and ready to break into triumphant laughter, as at last he was ready with his retort: "I knew ye—as well as he that made ye! Why, hear ye, my masters; was it for me to kill the heir apparent? Should I turn upon the true Prince?"

Whether this business was Owen's own, or Robert Taber's, or inherited from Samuel Phelps,* it is excellent; and it deserves to be set down in the margin of the actor's edition of the play. And there are countless other histrionic accretions which also demand to be preserved. Valuable as are Winter's and Booth's and Lewes' descriptions, Bell's record of Mrs. Siddons as Lady Macbeth and Mason's account of Salvini's Othello, they preserve for us only a few of the greater moments of a few of the greatest plays as performed by great actors.

We want more than this; we need to have in black and white the whole body of stage-tradition. We ought to have all the valuable readings and all the accessory business set down carefully and preserved permanently, for if these things are allowed to slip from the memory of the few who now know them, they can never be recovered. It may be admitted frankly that some of these traditions are incongruous excrescences, occasionally foolish and sometimes offensive, handed down thought-

* Sir Johnston Forbes-Robertson tells me that he does not recall it in Phelps' performance.

lessly from a time when the essential quality of Shakspere was less highly appreciated than it is today. There is no reason for regret, for instance, that the Second Gravedigger in 'Hamlet' no longer delays the action and disturbs the spirit of Ophelia's burial by stripping off an unexpected sequence of waistcoats to the delight of the unthinking—a clowning device which, oddly enough, is also traditional at the end of Molière's 'Précieuses Ridicules,' where it is not out of place since it is there quite in keeping with the tone of that lively little comedy. And perhaps there would be no loss if Romeo and Mercutio ceased to bewilder Peter when he is delivering the invitations by a succession of ironic salutations, just as Gratiano and Bassanio bewilder Gobbo,— the business being identical in both plays and having no warrant in the text of either.

These may be dismist as unwarrantable obtrusions to be discarded unhesitatingly; but to admit this is not to discredit the utility of the traditions in general. They are to be received as precious heirlooms, a legacy to the present and to the future, from the finest performers and from the most adroit stage-managers of the past, a store of accumulated devices always to be considered carefully, to be selected from judiciously and to be cast aside only after mature consideration. And, first of all, before any selection can be attempted, these traditions need all of them to be placed on record for what they are worth. Moreover, as the value of a suggestion, if not its validity, is due in part at least to the reputation of its suggester, the record ought (in so far as this is now possible) to register also the name of the originator of every specific piece of business and of every illuminating reading.

IV

JOHN PHILIP KEMBLE, for example, altho a little austere and chilly as an actor, was a most fertile deviser of points; and it is believed that some of the most striking effects made by Mrs. Siddons were due to the inventiveness of her brother. One of these, and one of the most characteristic, is in the trial scene of 'Henry VIII.' Queen Katharine comes before the King and the two cardinals, Wolsey and Campeius, sitting as judges of the legality of her marriage to Henry; and she begins by an appeal to her husband. When she makes an end, Wolsey, whom she knows for her personal enemy, counters by asserting the integrity and the learning of the judges of the case; and Campeius very courteously suggests that the royal session proceed. Then there follow these two speeches:

Queen.   Lord Cardinal,
               To you I speak.
Wolsey.   Your pleasure, madam.

But there are two cardinals present before her, and Campeius has just spoken. Why then should Wolsey alone answer when the Queen says,

Lord Cardinal, to you I speak?

The actress can, of course, suggest a sufficient reason for Wolsey's taking her words to himself by looking at him when she begins: yet this is barely sufficient, since the two cardinals are sitting side by side and the Queen is at some little distance. When Kemble played Wolsey and Mrs. Siddons was Queen Katharine this is how the brief dialog was managed. At the end of Campeius' sentence or two, the Queen spoke,

Lord Cardinal,

and then paused, whereupon Campeius rose and moved a little toward her, evidently believing that she was about to answer him. As he approacht her she turned from him impatiently, so Professor Bell has recorded, immediately making a sweet but dignified bow of apology. "Then to Wolsey, turned and looking from him, with her hand pointing back to him, in a voice of thunder,

To *you* I speak!

The effect of this outburst is so electric that it has been repeated in the subsequent revivals of 'Henry VIII,' as I can testify from my memory of Charlotte Cushman's performance, Modjeska's and Ellen Terry's; and in so arranging it Kemble made a permanent contribution to the staging of Shakspere."

As much cannot be said for an infelicitous invention of Sarah-Bernhardt's when she rashly ventured to exhibit herself as Hamlet. In the interview between Hamlet and the Queen in which he speaks daggers but uses none, he bids his mother contrast her two husbands:

Look here, upon this picture and on this.

How are those two portraits to be shown to the spectators? or are they to be shown at all? Henry Irving accepted them as purely imaginary, seen only in the mind's eye; and so did Edwin Booth sometimes, altho he often preferred to wear a miniature of his father, pendant from his neck so that he might compare this with a miniature of his uncle which his mother wore suspended also by a chain. Fechter tore the miniature of his uncle from the Queen's neck after contrasting it with a painting of his father hanging on the wall. Betterton had two half-length portraits side by side above the wainscot. Mme. Sarah-Bernhardt employed a pair of full-length paintings, framed high up in the woodwork on the wall facing the Queen as she sat; and when the young Prince expatiated piously on his father's qualities, physical and moral, the portrait of the elder Hamlet suddenly became transparent and thru it the audience beheld the Ghost—a trivial spectacular trick which immediately distracted the attention of the spectators.

Irving's suppression of visible portraits was perhaps more in accord with the spirit of the episode (and of the play as a whole) than was Booth's occasional use of two miniatures; certainly it was simpler. And yet Irving was rarely as simple as Booth. The American tragedian was wont to rely boldly on his mastery of the art of acting, whereas the British character-actor felt it advisable to support his impersonation by every possible device of the stage-manager. Irving may or may not have suspected the limitations of his accomplishment as an actor, whereas in stage-management his supremacy over all his contemporaries was indisputable. He was incessantly fertile and unfailingly dexterous in the discovery of novel methods for vivifying Shakspere's dialog. For the scene of Jessica's elopement in the 'Merchant of Venice' he designed a characteristic Venetian set—a piazzetta with Shylock's house on the right and with a bridge over the canal which crosses the stage. Shylock bids Jessica lock herself in; and then he goes away over the bridge to the supper to which he has been invited. It is the carnival season; and a merry band of maskers revels past with light laughter. Then Gratiano comes on; and a gondola glides up from which Lorenzo steps out. They hail Jessica, who throws to them out of the window her father's casket of jewels and money, after which she descends and unlocks the door, and comes out in boy's apparel, and lets her lover bear her away in the gondola. Gratiano remains and exchanges a few words with Antonio, who has chanced by. When they have gone, the maskers gaily flash across the bridge once more; and after a little the stage is left empty. Then in the distance we hear the tapping of Shylock's staff, and soon we see him crossing the bridge to stand at last knocking at the door of his now robbed and deserted home. It is only when he has knockt a second time that the curtain slowly falls, leaving us to imagine for ourselves his grief and his rage when he finds out his double misfortune.

Again in the trial-scene, after Shylock is baffled and despoiled, he asks leave to go.

I am not well. Send the deed after me, and I will sign it.

Irving made his exit and there was silence for a little space, suddenly broken by the angry murmurs of the mob outside, hooting at the discomfited usurer. For neither of these effects is there any warrant in Shakspere's text; the first was impossible on the sceneless stage of the Globe theater, and the second was too subtle for the ruder tastes of Tudor audiences; and yet both are perfectly in keeping with the temper and spirit of the play.

It is to be noted, however, that Irving missed a moving dramatic effect in allowing Ellen Terry to declaim the lines on the Quality of Mercy in

accord with the customary delivery of that ora-
tion, treating it as an eloquent opportunity for
triumphant elocution. Ada Rehan adjusted the
speech more artistically to the situation; Portia
has told Shylock that he must be merciful, and he
has scornfully askt,

On what compulsion must I?

Whereupon Portia explains to him the blessings
of mercy—and Ada Rehan then spoke the speech
as a summons to his better self, addressing herself
directly to him, evidently inspired by the hope
that her plea might soften his heart and watching
eagerly to discover if it did. Thus treated the
beautiful appeal intensified the dramatic poignancy of the moment; and thus treated it seems
to be more completely in harmony with Shakspere's intent.

Yet there is danger always in spending undue
effort in a vain attempt to discover what Shakspere or any other dramatist meant to do, instead
of centering our attention upon what he actually
did, whatever his intent may have been. It is
highly probable, for instance, that Shakspere
intended Shylock to be a despicable villain de-
testable to all spectators; but what Shakspere
actually did was to create an indisputable human
being, arousing our sympathy at the very time
when we hold him in horror. Fanny Kemble saw
Edmund Kean in 1827, and she recorded that he
"entirely divested Shylock of all poetry or eleva-

tion, but invested it with a concentrated ferocity that made one's blood curdle." Quite possibly all that Shakspere intended was this concentrated ferocity, but none the less did he lend poetry and elevation to the sinister character. Kean may have performed Shylock in accord with Shakspere's intent; but Irving and Booth, both of them, preferred to reveal rather the poetry and the elevation with which Shakspere had dowered the character. If Shylock has poetry and elevation, it is because Shakspere gave them to him, even if he knew not what he did; and it is always what the artist actually did, and not merely what he meant to do, which we need to perceive clearly.

Later generations read into a masterpiece of art many a meaning which the author might disclaim and yet which may be contained in it, none the less, because the great artist is great only because he has "builded better than he knew," even if he left latent what seem to us patent. A wide gulf yawns between us and our Tudor ancestors; and in the centuries that separate us there must have been many changes in taste, in opinion and in prejudice. To the stalwart and stout-stomached Elizabethans Shylock may have appeared as one kind of a creature, while he seems to us a very different being, more human mainly because we ourselves are more humane. Irving's pathetic return of Shylock to his abandoned home would have been hooted by the groundlings of the Globe;

and yet it is a pictorial embellishment which serves to bring out the Shylock whom we watch with commingled abhorrence and sympathy, even tho Shakspere might himself protest that sympathy should not be wasted on his sordid serio-comic villain.

V

IN its time Fechter's Hamlet was the cause of a plentiful waste of ink, let loose by the deliberate novelty of his performance. Fundamentally Fechter was an emotional rather than an intellectual actor; and what chiefly interested him in the tragedy was not so much the character of Hamlet as the swift succession of striking situations. To him the 'Hamlet' of Shakspere was like the 'Ruy Blas' of Victor Hugo, essentially a melodrama altho adorned with exquisite poetry—and there is this much to be said for Fechter's view, that we can still catch sight of the supporting skeleton of the coarser tragedy-of-blood which Shakspere endowed with the humanity of a true tragedy. Where English actors had been a little inclined to see an embodiment of philosophic reflection, sicklied o'er with the pale cast of thought, the French actor saw a romantic hero entangled in a complexity of pathetic situations; and what interested him was rather the theatrical effectiveness of these situations than the soul of the hero himself. To Fech-

123

ter, Hamlet was a picturesque part for the leading man of the Porte Saint Martin; and he naturally treated the play as he would treat any other Porte Saint Martin melodrama, to be made as emotionally effective as might be and to be presented as pictorially as possible.

As Hamlet was a Dane, Fechter presented him as a blond, adorning his head with locks not exactly flaxen in tint but rather reddish. (On this point doubt is not possible since the wig that Fechter used to wear as Hamlet is now piously preserved among the other histrionic memorabilia on exhibition in the club-house of The Players in New York.) Himself a sculptor in his youth and always closely associated with artists pictorial and plastic, Fechter was fertile in designing the scenic habiliment of the plays he produced. A large part of the action of 'Hamlet' was made to take place in the main hall of the castle of Elsinore. In this spacious room we saw the performance of the 'Mousetrap' and also the fencing match of the final act. This hall filled the stage; it had broad doors at the back, and above this portal was a gallery with smaller doors at both ends leading off to upper rooms and with curving stairways descending on either side. Many of the exits and entrances were made by means of one or another of these stairways; and Fechter utilized them artfully when the time came for the killing of the King. The throne upon

which Claudius sat to behold the fencing was on
one side. Kate Field's record of the business,
in her biography of Fechter, conforms to my own
recollection of it:—

"The moment Hamlet exclaimed

> Ho! let the door be lockt.
> Treachery! Seek it out!

"the King exhibited signs of fear; and while
Laertes made his terrible confession, the regicide
stole to the opposite stairs, shielding himself
from Hamlet's observation behind a group of
courtiers who, paralized with horror, failed to
remark the action. Laertes no sooner uttered
the words

> The King's to blame!

than Hamlet turned suddenly to the throne in
search of his victim. Discovering the ruse he
rushed up the left-hand stairs, to meet the King
in the center of the gallery and stabbed him.
" . . . As he descended the stairs the potent
poison stole upon Hamlet, who, murmuring

> The rest is silence!

fell dead upon the corpse of Laertes, thus showing his forgiveness of treachery and remembrance
of Ophelia."

125

VI

MENTION has already been made of Ada Rehan's method of delivering the appeal to Shylock's better nature in which she described the quality of mercy. In default of evidence I cannot say whether her attitude was derived from a tradition which had not been preserved in such other performances of the 'Merchant of Venice' as I have been permitted to see, or whether it was assumed for the first time in Augustin Daly's last production of the play. Daly was a producer—to use the term now accepted in the theater—of singular individuality, familiar with accepted traditions, and yet often preferring to discard them in favor of novelties of his devising. On occasion he exhibited a wrongheadness which was almost perverse in its eccentricity; but far more frequently his originality manifested itself in unhackneyed arrangements which set familiar passages in a new light.

Of all his Shaksperian revivals the 'Taming of the Shrew' was perhaps the most completely satisfying in its sumptuous stage-setting and in its intricate stage-management, yet his presentation of 'As You Like It' was a close second. As he was a martinet in the discipline of his company, we may credit to him rather than to the actor himself a new departure in the interpretation of the character of Jaques. In the structure of

'As You Like It' Shakspere closely followed the story of Lodge's 'Rosalynde'; yet he introduced several figures not to be found in this source. One of these is Jaques, who has nothing whatever to do with the plot of the piece, who seems to exist for his own sake, and who is allowed to usurp the attention of the audience for his self-revelatory harangues. I have suggested elsewhere that possibly Jaques was invented for the sole purpose of providing a part for Burbage —a part rich in elocutionary opportunities. Now, what manner of man is this Jaques, created to disclose himself not by action but only by discourse?

Richard Grant White maintained "that what Jaques meant by melancholy was what we now call cynicism—a sullen, scoffing, snarling spirit." In the view of the American critic, Jaques "was one of those men who believe in nothing good, and who as the reason of their lack of faith in human nature and of hope of human happiness, and their want of charity, tell us that they have seen the world." White declared that in delivering the speech on the seven ages of man, Jaques seizes "the occasion to sneer at the representatives of the whole human race."

For this opinion of Jaques the critic claimed originality for himself, asserting that it was contrary to that usually shown on the stage. Since White first stated it in 1854, it has succeeded in acclimating itself in the theater, where Jaques has frequently been presented as an embittered despiser of mankind; in fact, it bids fair to establish itself as the accepted stage-tradition. This reading of the part is attractive to the actor of Jaques, since it increases the wilful perversity of his personality and makes the character stand out in bold relief, his malignity contrasting with the kindliness of the Duke and of his genial companions in the forest.

But is this necessarily the right reading of the part? Is there ever any one interpretation of the more richly rounded characters of Shakspere's plays which we must accept as undeniably the only admissible rendering? In his more ambitious figures Shakspere is not satisfied to give us mere outlines, profiles, silhouettes, to be seen from one angle only; he bestows upon them the rotundity of real life; and we may dispute about them, as we dispute about the characters of our acquaintances and of prominent men in public life. No critic may feel entitled to assert that he has attained to a final decision as to the exact character of Hamlet or Shylock or Jaques; and every one of us is justified in defending his own opinion as to these creatures of imagination all compact.

Certainly it was a Jaques very unlike White's that Daly showed us in his revival of 'As You Like It.' Daly held that Jaques is a humorist, recognized as such by all his comrades—a humorist who affects to be a satirist and who is not to be taken too seriously. And Jaques himself is quite conscious of this tolerant and amused attitude of his fellows toward him and that they are always expecting him to take antagonistic views and are always wondering what he is going to say next, ever ready for his exaggerated outbreaks and ever ready to laugh with him, even if they are also laughing at him. As Jaques is aware of their expectation, he responds to it; he gives them what they are looking for; he abounds in his own sense; he looses free rein to his wit and to his whimsical fantasy, certain that his customary hearers will know that there is no sting to his satire. Such men are not uncommon nowadays in real life; and in the threatening monotony of our modern existence they are eagerly welcomed and their over-emphatic utterances are awaited with smiling expectancy.

It was thus that Daly conceived the character of Jaques and that he arranged the way in which the other actors should receive the outpourings of the self-conscious humorist. When Orlando breaks in upon the feast and demands food for Adam, the Duke bids him go and fetch the faithful old servant. The interval between Orlando's departure and his return with Adam must be filled up so that the audience may not be forced to feel that it has been kept waiting; and Shak-

spere drafts Jaques for this service. After Orlando goes, the Duke remarks that

> We are not all alone unhappy.
> This wide and universal theater
> Presents more woful pageants than the scene
> Wherein we play in.

Here Jaques sees his opportunity and declares
that

> All the world's a stage,
> And all the men and women merely players.

Then he pauses, to observe whether this meets
with approval; and the others smile back, as if
to encourage him to proceed. Thus heartened
by their sympathetic attention he takes up his
parable and evolves the theory of the seven ages
of man. He is not reciting a set speech, prepared
in advance; he is extemporizing, sometimes
hesitating for the right word, and always acutely
sensitive to the effect he is producing upon his
listeners. Thus delivered the speech is robbed
of its bitterness and emptied of its cynicism.
And as it falls from the lips of Jaques its hearers
exchange glances in recognition of the fact that
their humorous friend is in excellent vein, surpassing himself in whimsical exaggeration, even
if he ends, as humorists are wont to do, upon a
note of melancholy.

When the familiar words are spoken under these conditions they have a freshness which is totally absent if Jaques declaims them as part of a set speech. In his illuminating address on the 'Illusion of the First Time in Acting,' William Gillette* has dwelt on the danger to which the drama is exposed whenever the actor carelessly reveals himself as knowing by heart the words which the character is supposed to be uttering without premeditation. There is always a temptation for the performer to see in the Seven Ages and the Quality of Mercy, in Hamlet's soliloquy and Mark Antony's appeal, an opportunity for an elocutionary exhibition, perhaps effective enough in itself, yet damaging to the total effect of the play. To turn every one of these speeches into a piece to be spoken may not be fairly described as a stage-tradition; yet the practice is far too prevalent in the acting of Shakspere to-day, and it is probably an inheritance from the past. There would be a stimulus to the adoption of a better method if the actor's edition of Shakspere should record the various devices by which this danger has been averted.

In this paper it has been possible to adduce only

* It may be noted that Gillette's address and the essays of Coquelin and Fleeming Jenkin, from which quotation has been made in this paper, are all reprinted in the Second Series of the Publications of the Dramatic Museum of Columbia University (1915).

a few of the many instances where an unexpected
illumination of Shakspere's text has been accomplisht by inventive actors and by ingenious
stage-managers, who have made explicit what
they believed to be implicit in the dialog. Where
they found only the seed itself, they have shown
the expanding flower potentially contained within
it. What they have done for Shakspere they have
done for Molière and for Sheridan; and this is
one reason why the accredited classics of the
drama are likely to seem to us, when we see them
on the stage, ampler in detail and solider in texture
than the plays of our own time, which have not yet
been able to profit by the contributions of generation after generation of actors and stage-managers.
And a warm welcome awaits the editor who shall
employ the most significant of these stage-tradi-
tions to vivify the text of his edition of Shakspere.

(1916.)

VII

THE PLEASANT LAND OF SCRIBIA

I

AS we look down the long history of dramatic literature we cannot help seeing that the successful playwrights may be assorted into different groups. They are all of them, of course, first and foremost playwrights—that is to say, they all possess the innate and instinctive gift of arousing and of retaining the interest of the playgoers of their own time and of their own country. They are all story-tellers on the stage, because a play needs a plot above all else, if it is to please long and to please many. But the kind of story they will select and the degree of importance they will give to the story itself will depend on their own differing attitude toward life and their own special qualifications.

Some successful playwrights are poets, essentially dramatic, like Sophocles and Shakspere, or essentially lyric like Rostand and d'Annunzio. Some are social satirists, like Molière and Beaumarchais. Some are wits like Sheridan or humorists like Labiche. Some, like Ibsen, are primarily psychologists creating characters to be revealed in successive situations; and some, like Brieux, are sociologists dealing with the problems of the day. Some are journalists, as Aristophanes was on occasion and as Sardou was in his earlier comedies of contemporary Paris. Some are preachers, like Bernard Shaw. And some of them are simply story-tellers, pure and simple, not poets or psychologists or philosophers, not humorists or journalists, but merely concocters of plots, so adroitly put together that the acted narratives amuse us in the playhouse and give us the special pleasure to be found only in the theater, without providing us with the added delight which we derive from the veracious and significant portrayal of men and women.

Of these story-tellers of the stage, content to be story-tellers only and satisfied to rely on the attraction of a sequence of ingenious situations artfully articulated, Scribe is the chief. He is not a poet; he is not even a man of letters; he does not make us think; he does not deposit in our memories anything worthy of remembrance. All he can do is to amuse us while we are in the playhouse with the mechanical dexterity of the story he is setting before us by the aid of all the devices of the theater. He is a story-teller on the stage and nothing else; but he is one of the indisputable masters of stage story-telling. His stories may be empty, arbitrary, artificial; but they are sufficient unto themselves. He is successful in achieving all that he is ambitious of attaining—the entertainment of the spectators, by the exhibition of his surpassing skill in inventing and in combining effective situations.

It may be admitted that merely as a craftsman he is not more dexterous than certain of the greater dramatists. As sheer machinery nothing of his is better in its kind than the exposition of 'Othello' or of 'Tartuffe'; and he never put together a plot more artistically wrought out than those of 'Œdipus the King' or of 'Ghosts.' But Shakspere and Molière, Sophocles and Ibsen, while they reveal themselves as the most accomplisht of technicians, are not content to be technicians only and the larger, loftier and nobler qualities of their dramas are so abundantly evident that few of us ever pay attention to their marvelous mastery of technic. But Scribe was nothing but a technician; and it is solely by his mastery of technic that he maintained himself in the theater for two score years.

He was astonishingly fertile; and his productivity was exhibited in almost every department of the drama,—in farce, in the comedy of anecdote, in opéra-comique, in grand opera, and even in librettos for the ballet. He did not lay his scenes always in his native land, whose manners and customs he could not help knowing; at one time or another he ventured to manufacture plots supposed to take place in almost every habitable country in the globe. The 'Bataille de Dames' and 'Adrienne Lecouvreur' were stories of France; but the action of the 'Dame Blanche' took place in Scotland, that of 'Fra Diavolo' in Italy, that of 'La Juive' in Spain, that of 'Le Prophète' in Germany, and that of 'L'Africaine' partly in Africa. In one piece, suggested by Fenimore Cooper's 'Lionel Lincoln,' he even ventured to cross the western ocean and to take Boston for his background.

Sometimes, as in the case of the Cooper adaptation and of the 'Dumb Girl of Portici' he had to go abroad because the original of the story he was setting on the stage was foreign and could not well be made French. And sometimes, on the other hand, he transported his tale to a far country, to a land other than his own, so that he could attribute to it the manners and the customs and the laws which he needed to enable him to immesh the puppets of his plot in the thrilling situations he had invented. He did not set out on these travels to capture the local color of the countries he might visit, as Hugo had essayed to do in 'Hernani' and in 'Ruy Blas.' Scribe's local color was always sporadic and superficial. He went far afield in order to profit by conditions different from those familiar to French playgoers; and these conditions were not necessarily those which actually obtained in the foreign parts to which he exiled the personages of his plays;

they were those which he needed to bring about the events he was devising. Therefore the manners and the customs and the laws which we find in many of the stories of Scribe set before us on the stage are not really those of Spain or Italy, of England or Germany, of Africa or America; they were in fact almost as much Scribe's own invention as the stories themselves.

II

SCRIBE's frequent departures from the facts of history and of geography were promptly noted by contemporary critics more familiar with foreign lands than he was; and they accused him of having imagined a country of his own, to which they gave his name—La Scribie—Scribia—a very useful country for a playwright because its social conventions existed solely for the playwright's convenience and because they might be modified unceasingly as the exigencies of plot making demanded. When Andrew Lang first heard of this fabled domain, he was moved to the composition of a lyric, which he called 'Partant pour la Scribie.'

A pleasant land is Scribie, where
The light comes mostly from below,
And seems a sort of symbol rare
Of things at large, and how they go.

137

In rooms where doors are everywhere
　And cupboards shelter friend and foe.

＊　＊　＊　＊　＊　＊　＊　＊

A land of lovers false and gay;
　A land where people dread a curse;
A land of letters gone astray,
　Or intercepted, which is worse;
Where weddings false fond maids betray,
　And all the babes are changed at nurse.

＊　＊　＊　＊　＊　＊　＊　＊

Oh, happy land, where things come right
　We, of the world where things go ill;
Where lovers love, but don't unite;
　Where no one finds the Missing Will—
Dominion of the heart's delight,
　Scribie, we've loved, and love thee still!

Unfortunately the lyrist who rimed this delectable description had allowed himself to be deceived by a traveler's tale rarely to be relied upon. The land for which he has here exprest his longing is not the true Scribia, as this is accurately mapped on the atlas of imaginary geography. It is an adjoining territory first explored by Jerome K. Jerome and explained in his authoritative book of travels, entitled 'Stage-Land, Curious Habits and Customs of its Inhabitants.' Among the many citizens of this peculiar place whom Jerome was enterprizing enough to interview, were the Stage-Hero and his fit mate, the Stage-Heroine, the Stage-Villain, and the Stage-Adventuress, the Stage-Detective and the Stage-Lawyer.

Mr. Jerome was able to accompany his analysis of these peculiar personalities by an account of the legislation which governs their conduct and which has hitherto been unfamiliar to students of comparative jurisprudence. It appears that in Stage-Land, when a man dies, without leaving a will, then all his property goes to the nearest villain. But, if the deceased has left a will, then and in that case, all his property goes to the person who can get possession of this document. As Jerome fails to cite any decisions in support of these laws, we are left to infer that they are statutory and not judge-made. Yet he is frank to inform us that he has not been able to ascertain the fundamental principles of the jurisprudence of Stage-Land, since "fresh acts and clauses and modifications appear to be introduced for each new play"; and here we discover a condition of things closely resembling that which obtains in Scribia.

Yet Stage-Land is not Scribia, altho their several populations are apparently descended from the same stock. It is in Stage-Land rather than in Scribia, that the Missing Will always turns up in the nick of time and that all the babes are changed at nurse. Nor is Scribia identical, as some geographers seem to have believed, with the No Man's Land in which dwelt the pale personages of M. Maeterlinck's earlier plays, a shadowy and mysterious realm where the unsubstantial 'Intruder' finds his way invisibly into the household of death and where the 'Sightless' wander aimlessly and hopelessly. Still less is Scribia to be confounded with two other countries, Utopia and Altruria, about which the gazetteers are able to supply us only with pitiably insufficient information. There is, however, a certain plausibility in the suggestion that Scribia has for its capital the city of Weiss-nicht-wo and that it has recently rectified its frontiers by annexing the contiguous principality of Zenda.

When Brunetière was bringing to its logical conclusion his illuminating series of lectures on the evolution of French dramatic literature, he took as the topics for his final talk Scribe and Alfred de Musset, contemporary and unlike—Scribe the craftsman who was only a craftsman thinking solely of the theater and living in it contentedly, and Musset the lyrist, careless of formal structure and regardless of the narrowing limitations of the playhouse. Different as they were in equipment and in aim, both of them were wont to take for the scene of their dissimilar dramas, emptily prosaic in the one case and in the other abundantly poetic, the non-existent country, which had been named after the elder of them, and which was a land of fantasy with manners and laws easy to manipulate according to the necessities of the fables they had taken as the foundations of their pieces. Brunetière did not call Scribia by its name; but he did draw the attention of his hearers to the ideal Bavaria of Musset's 'Fantasio,' the Italy of his 'Bettine,' the Sicily of his 'Carmosine' and the Hungary of his 'Barberine'—"all Shaksperian lands, if I may so call them, in which characters from fairy-tales undergo their adventures in gardens always in bloom and under skies that are eternally blue."

III

WHEN Brunetière ventured to suggest that the indeterminate backgrounds of Musset's ironic imaginations might be called Shaksperian, he was only recognizing the obvious fact that the French lyrist, alone among modern dramatists, had chosen to follow in the footsteps of the author of 'As You Like It' and of 'Twelfth Night.' From Shakspere Musset borrowed the commingling of realistic and prosaic characters with characters poetic and romanticized. He arbitrarily banisht the persons who people his airy fantasies to a far and foreign land chiefly that he might let them live in an atmosphere of remoteness and enable them to escape from the limitations and the rigors of commonplace existence in contemporary Paris. So Shakspere, in order that an unknown distance from London might lend enchantment to the view, had chosen to domicile the grave and the gay characters of his romantic comedies in a Bohemia which is a desert country by the sea and in a Forest of Arden where glide gilded snakes and where roam lions with udders all drawn dry.

No doubt Musset scorned Scribe as bitterly as did his fellow lyrist, Heine; and he was almost the only French dramatist of his day who was not tempted to emulate the tricky dexterity of Scribe; but none the less do we find many of his creatures living in the pleasant land of Scribia—just as many of Shakspere's lighter characters had resided in the same strange country more than two centuries earlier. And while Musset knew about Scribe even if he might detest him and all his works, Shakspere could have had no foreknowledge of the prolific French playmaker whose productivity was to manifest itself more than two centuries after that of the English dramatist had ceased. Still it is difficult to deny that Shakspere, who may never have set foot outside of his precious isle set in the silver sea, had let his fancy transport him to a territory which we can now recognize as the Scribia known to all students of the French dramatists of the nineteenth century.

It is not from any actual Verona in any actual Italy, but from a town of the same name in the heart of Scribia, that two gentlemen departed one after another, destined to show once more that the course of false love does not always run smooth. It is in a Scribian and not in an Italian Venice, where dwelt a Jewish usurer who was trickt out of the deadly forfeit set down in his merry bond by the sharp practice of a quick-witted woman triumphantly passing herself off as a lawyer. In fact, the administration of justice in this fabled Venice is so frankly fantastic and so completely contrary to all the precedents which would govern the courts of any actual Venice, that we find ourselves wondering whether this imagined city in the sea is situated in Scribia or in the adjacent realm of Stage-Land explored and described by Mr. Jerome.

Again it is in Scribia and not in Greece that the Athens stood whose Duke wooed and won the Queen of the Amazons, while the British-born Bottom, after marvelous misadventures due to the malice of a fairy King, made ready with his mates to perform a lamentable tragedy at the ducal bridal ceremony. Where except upon the coast of Scribia could we find the Ephesus, the laws of which put the obtruding stranger immediately on trial for his life and the magic atmosphere of which made it possible for twins separated in infancy and brought up in widely parted places to be in manhood indistinguishable one from the other in speech and even in costume? And where, except off the coast of Scribia, could that enchanted isle lie which was full of disheartening noises and which was suddenly invaded by a ship's company cast up by the sea as the result of an artificial tempest raised by the cunning of a royal magician.

Students of imaginary geography, aware that Utopia was discovered and described by More in 1516 and that the earliest tidings from Altruria were brought by a traveler interviewed by Howells in 1894, have never had occasion to question the discovery of Scribia in the first half of the nineteenth century, during the lifetime of the man from whom it took its name. Yet we can now perceive that this pleasant land was not unknown to Shakspere in the first half of the seventeenth century, and that he profited hugely by his information as to its manners, its customs and its laws, finding them modifiable to suit his convenience. How is this to be explained?

After long meditation over all the peculiarities of this problem I am emboldened to proffer a solution, suggested by the notorious fact that history is prone to repeat itself. This solution I venture to submit herewith to the charitable judgment of experts in imaginary geography. Altho Scribia has been a densely populated realm since a time whereof the memory of man runneth not to the contrary, and altho it had been visited and traverst and dwelt in by many of the characters of Shakspere and a little later by not a few of the characters of Beaumont and Fletcher, for some inexplicable reason it had failed to be described in any gazetteer of literature; and at some unknown date it seems to have secluded itself and forbidden the entry of all foreigners, just as Japan chose to shut itself off from the rest of the world.

After long scores of years it was rediscovered by Scribe, colonized by his characters, reintroduced into the community of nations and named anew. It is to be regretted that there is never any hope of rectifying an error in geographic nomenclature; and as this western continent will continue to hear the name not of Columbus, but of Americus Vespucius, so to the end of time will Scribia commemorate the ingenious industry of Eugene Scribe, falsely believed to be its original discoverer. And here, to companion the lilting lyric of Andrew Lang is a copy of verses by Charles Godfrey Leland:

> Thru years of toil, Columbus
>   Unto our New World came;
> But a charlatan skipt after,
>   And gave that world his name.
>
> All day in street and market
>   The liar's name we see;

Columbia !—sweet and seldom—
  Is left to Poetry.

And the names bring back a lesson
  Taught to the world in youth—
That the realm of Song and Beauty
  Is the only home of Truth.

(1918.)

VIII

'HAMLET' WITH HAMLET LEFT OUT*

I

IN the flotsam and jetsam of theatrical anecdote, derived from the wreckage of forgotten books of histrionic biography, no tale is more familiar than that which records how a strolling company playing a one-night stand and unexpectedly maimed by the illness of its leading actor, ventured nevertheless to perform the play it had promised with a modification of the original advertisement to accord with the unfortunate fact. That is to say, the company declared its intention of performing "the play of 'Hamlet'— with the part of Hamlet left out."

Despite diligent endeavor I have not been able to discover where or when this fabled performance was believed to have taken place. Still less successful have I been in my search for one of the spectators at this unique representation of Shakspere's masterpiece. It would be both pleasant and profitable if only a single survivor of the

* This paper was read before the Modern Language Association of America, at Columbia University, in December, 1914.

audience on that occasion could be interrogated as to the impression produced upon him by the tragedy thus bereft of its central figure. With Hamlet himself subtracted, what can be left? The scene in which Polonius loads his son with excellent advice, the scene of Ophelia's madness, and the scene of the two grave-diggers,—these would remain intact, and little more. The rest is silence.

There is perhaps no other play of Shakspere's (not even 'Macbeth') in which the title-part is as integrally related to almost every episode of the plot as it is in 'Hamlet.' It would not be difficult to arrange an acting edition of both halves of 'Henry IV' with the part of Henry IV left out, for we should still have Prince Hal and Falstaff and all their jovial crew. And it would not be impossible, altho the feat would demand the utmost dramaturgic dexterity, to prepare a theatrically effective version of 'Julius Cæsar' with the part of Julius Cæsar left out. As a matter of fact not a few critics have complained that Julius Cæsar does not bulk big enough in the tragedy which bears his name; and by this complaint these critics revealed that they were unfamiliar with the custom of the Tudor theater which prescribed the giving of the name of the sovran to any historical play dealing with his times, even if he himself might not be a dominating personality in its story.

But even if Julius Cæsar and Henry IV are not the most important or the most interesting characters in the plays named after them, at least they do take part in the action from time to time. They pass across the stage at intervals and are seen by the spectators. Neither Shakspere nor any other Elizabethan dramatist ever dreamed of so constructing a piece as to center attention on an important and interesting character who should not be brought bodily on the stage. The Tudor relish for the concrete was too intense for the playgoers to accept etherial subtleties of this sort; and the playwright himself was necessarily the contemporary of the playgoers, sharing in their simple tastes and in their bold desires. Even the frequent ghosts who stalk thru Shakspere's tragedies were on his stage boldly visible specters, white-sheeted and gory-throated,—these very ghosts which a stage-manager today delicately suggests by ingenious scientific devices or less confidently leaves to the imagination of the spectators.

It is curious that the Elizabethan audiences, perfectly willing to imagine scenery at the will of the author, demanded to see every character in the drama, standing on the stage and speaking for himself, whereas the spectators of today, insisting upon an adequate scenic background for every episode of the play are willing enough to imagine a character who never appears before

149

their eyes,—an unseen personage who may indeed be more important and more interesting than any other personage who actually stands in front of them on the stage.

II

In a volume of one-act plays composed by a young American playwright, George Middleton, there is a piece called 'Their Wife,' in which the most significant figure is that of the woman who has been the wife of one man and who is the wife of another. The only two characters who are seen and heard by the audience are these two husbands; their wife does not appear; and yet she is the heroine of the play. It is solely because she is what she is that the action of the piece is possible; and it is her character which is the core of the situation wherein the two men find themselves entangled. We do not see her in the flesh, but the dramatist has made us see her in the spirit. He has interpreted her thru the mouths of the two men who have loved her and whom she has loved in turn. She is the most clearly depicted person in the play, so clearly depicted, indeed, that the spectator realizes her for what she is. Oddly enough a little later or a little earlier Mr. George Ade had made use of exactly the same device in his one-act play 'Nettie,' in which we are made to see the invisible heroine as she has imprest herself on three of her "gentle-men-friends." Quite possibly an average unobservant playgoer, recalling one or the other of these plays after an interval of a month or two, could discuss its heroine so oblivious of the fact that he had not actually seen her, that he might find himself endeavoring vainly to remember the name of the actress who played the part.

It is now nearly half-a-century since Sardou brought out one of the cleverest of his satiric comedies, the 'Famille Benoiton.' It dealt with the fortunes of a family in the second decade of the Second Empire, with its gaudy glitter and with its gangrene of social disintegration. Monsieur and Madame Benoiton have sons and daughters, married, marriageable, and not yet ripe for matrimony. All the members of the family are presented to us in turn, singly and together,—all of them except Madame Benoiton. They are put thru their paces in a series of amusing scenes; and we discover slowly that the family is in its sorry state, largely because it lacks the guiding hand of the mother. Madame Benoiton is never at home; she may have just gone out or she may be immediately expected; but she does not appear with the rest of the family. She is a woman of fashion, or she aspires so to be considered; and her "social duties" are too absorbing for her to give any time to her husband, to her sons or to her daughters.

When at last the fifth act draws to its conclusion, with the reconciliation of the eldest daughter to her husband and with the engagement of the next oldest daughter to an eligible bachelor, there is the sound of carriage-wheels and a ring at the front door. The youngest boy looks out the window, cries "Mamma!" and rushes away to greet her. The eligible bachelor smiles with anticipatory delight; he has yet to be introduced to his future mother-in-law! Then the boy returns disappointed; and when he is askt where his mother is, he explains that she has just gone out again:—"She had forgotten her parasol!"

Here again quite possibly the average unobservant playgoer, recalling the play after an interval, might easily fail to remember that he had never laid eyes on Madame Benoiton herself, altho it was because she was what she was that her children had developed into the characters set before us. Quite possibly once more Sardou himself, intent only upon a characteristically clever theatrical trick, did not intend or even apprehend the full significance of Madame Benoiton's absence from the home which it was her privilege to control. Yet his technical skill was sufficient to impress upon us a clear vision of this unseen mother, derelict to her duty.

It deserves to be recorded also that in Alphonse Daudet's play of Provençal life, 'L'Arlé-

sienne,' the woman of Arles, who is the cause of
the fatal catastrophe, does not appear before
the eyes of the spectators.

III

It may not be strictly accurate to say that in
Ibsen's 'Rosmersholm' the mainspring of the
action is Beata, Rosmer's wife, who had thrown
herself into the stream some time before the
opening scene of the play. In fact, such an assertion would be inexact, since it is the scheming of
Rebecca West which has brought about Beata's
suicide. Yet the dead Beata is as determining
a figure upon the action of 'Rosmersholm' as
the dead Julius Cæsar is upon that part of the
action of 'Julius Cæsar' which follows his assassination. Here again it is because Beata was
what she was that the ambition of Rebecca West
to take her place came so near to fulfilment.
And it is with marvelous adroitness that Ibsen
drops the hints and supplies the suggestions here
and there which we eagerly piece together (much
as we might work over the once popular puzzle-
pictures) until at last we are enabled to make out
a full-length portrait of the dead and gone wife,
whose gentle spirit is now more potent over the
volitions of her husband and of the woman who
aspires to be her successor than it was while
she was yet on earth to mingle with them, a

153

pale and unobtrusive figure. It is the influence emanating from Beata which really inhibits Rebecca from the accomplishment of her intent to marry Beata's widower.

In two of Sir Arthur Pinero's plays there are also dead wives, whose personality reaches forward and interferes with the orderly march of events after their departure from this life. In the 'Second Mrs. Tanqueray' we are made to feel the austere chilliness of the first Mrs. Tanqueray, her cold-blooded physical asceticism, which ultimately drove the warm-blooded widower to ask the equally warm-blooded Paula to become his second wife. And in 'His House in Order' we are presented with a second wife tormented by the saintly reputation of the first wife, to whose memory everything is sacrificed including the happiness of her successor. The culminating moment of the play is when the outraged second wife discovers that this saintly reputation of the first wife was usurpt, since the dead woman had been unfaithful. It must be admitted that the author has not been as skilful or at least not as successful in 'His House in Order' as in the 'Second Mrs. Tanqueray' in creating in our minds a distinct impression of the unseen woman whose dead hand clutches the heart of the action. The first Mrs. Tanqueray we can reconstruct sharply enough. But the first wife of the man whose house is not in order remains a rather unsatisfactory shadow, since it is a little difficult for us to perceive exactly how it was that a woman of her indefensible character should have been able to pass as a woman of her indisputable reputation.

IV

In these two plays by Sir Arthur Pinero as well as in the 'Rosmersholm' of Ibsen, dead women still influence the lives of living men; even tho they are dead when the several plays begin, they had each of them been alive only a little while earlier, a few months or a few years. In one of Maeterlinck's somber pieces, remote from the realities and the trivialities of everyday existence, there is also a personage unseen by the spectators, a personage not dead, since he never had been alive in the flesh.

In the 'Intruder,' Maeterlinck invites us to behold a dim hall in which a waiting family is gathered, grandfather, father, daughters, children—all but the mother who lies in the adjoining room, desperately ill and hovering between life and death. The conversation between the different members of the family is subdued and almost in whispers. The blind grandfather hears a step in the garden outside;—but nobody has come to the gate. A moment later he hears the click of the latch of the gate, as if it had opened

and shut;—but nobody has past thru. Then
the old man asks who has entered the room:—
but nobody has been seen to come in. And as
query follows query, the spectators begin to
suspect that the senses of the blind man are super-
normally acute and that he is conscious of happenings which the others fail to perceive. The
dialog is as tense as it is terse; it is all in question and answer; it abounds in seemingly unmeaning repetition which the audience feels
somehow to be strangely significant. There is
an almost breathless suspense while we wonder
whether or not there is an invisible visitor and
while we ask ourselves who this unseen newcomer
can be. Finally the door of the sick room
opens and the sister of charity, who has been
in attendance on the ailing mother, is seen standing silent with hands crost over her breast. Then
at last we know with certainty that there was a
mysterious visitor and that he was no less a
person than Death himself.

Of all Maeterlinck's dramas the 'Intruder'
is perhaps the simplest in its story as it is the
strongest in its effect. And the means whereby
this effect is achieved are seemingly as simple as
the story itself. But altho the dramatist has
wisely chosen a primitive and elementary form,
he reveals his possession of the power to excite
the imagination and to make the spectators interpret for themselves what he had refrained from

bringing before their eyes. Often in poetry we discover that the part is greater than the whole; and in the 'Intruder' we perceive that the poet has so toucht the chords of our sensibilities that we attain to a vision of the whole, altho no part has actually been before our eyes. Here is a case where M. Maeterlinck was happily inspired, lighting on a topic which responded sympathetically to his etheriality of treatment. In the intangible means whereby an indefinable mood is evoked and sustained, there is nothing in modern literature comparable with the 'Intruder'— except, it may be, the 'Fall of the House of Usher,' where we find the same haunting and insistent melancholy, the same twilight paleness, the same dread advance of we know not what.

V

THE 'Intruder' differs from the several plays in which there is an absent character in that even the most careless and oblivious spectator must recall the fact that the grisly invader was not seen by anyone either in the auditorium or on the stage. In this play we have no true parallel to 'Hamlet' with the part of Hamlet left out because we have been made to feel that Death has actually past before us even if our eyes have proved too feeble to perceive him. He is a thing unseen; yet the accumulated evidence is too convincing for us to dream of denying his actual presence. There is, however, another French play in which a character actually alive, altho far distant, is the motive force of the action of a play wherein he has not appeared and in which his name is only casually mentioned.

This is the 'Death of the Duke of Enghien' by Léon Hénnique, a brief tragedy in three swift episodes. In the first we are shown the headquarters of the French general in command at Strasburg; and to him an officer brings orders for a raid into neutral territory to capture the Duke. The obedient general does not discuss or dispute this command; but the spectators feel that he does not approve it. In the second part we see the Duke at Ettenheim, in the midst of his little court. While they are at table, the house is surrounded by the French cavalry. The general enters and arrests the Duke by the order of the French First Consul. In the third scene we behold the sitting of the court-martial in a dilapidated room in the castle of Vincennes. There are no witnesses against the Duke, no incriminating papers, no counsel for the defense; yet these things are disregarded without comment. The Duke is summoned and interrogated with the utmost courtesy. He scorns to deny that he has fought against the Republic. Thereupon the members of the military tribunal withdraw to deliberate—but the spectators are never in doubt as to the fatal verdict. In time the Duke drops off to sleep, to be awakened by an officer who bids him summon his courage and follow. When he has gone the audience overhears the sentence read to him as he stands in the moat below the open window. Then comes the order to fire, and with the rattle of musketry the curtain slowly descends.

Nothing can be barer than the dialog of this drama; it achieves the acme of directness; and in the trial scene almost every word is derived from the official report. The name of the First Consul is not brought in; and yet the author has made the spectators feel that it is the steel volition of Napoleon which commands every movement and which dictates every word. It is a duel to the death between the two, the captive whom we behold and the implacable usurper who overrules justice to destroy a man he wishes out of the way. It is a duel of an unarmed man with an unseen opponent, for the final thrust of whose long rapier there is no possible parry. Napoleon pervades the whole play from the beginning to the end; he is the hero-villain; his iron will is the mainspring of the action; and we cannot fail to feel this altho he never comes before us and altho no one dares to bring in his name.

In the 'Marion Delorme' of Victor Hugo it is the inflexible determination of Richelieu which controls the action. Altho the Cardinal is never seen, yet he is heard to utter a single word, "No!" from behind the curtains of his litter as he is borne across the stage in the final act. In Hénnique's play Napoleon is neither seen nor heard, nor is his name bandied about as is Richelieu's in Hugo's drama. Surely here at last is a novelty in the drama; here is really an analog to the performance of 'Hamlet' with the part of Hamlet left out. Still the student of the stage will not readily admit that any novelty is possible at this late date in the long history of the theater; and with no very great difficulty he can recall at least one drama in which there is a single combat between a character whom the spectators can see and sympathize with and an unseen personality of inflexible determination. The 'Death of the Duke of Enghien' is comparatively recent, since it was acted in Paris in the later years of the nineteenth century; and yet it was anticipated in Athens more than two thousand years ago by the earliest of the Greek dramatic poets.

In the 'Prometheus Bound' of Æschylus the play begins with the rivetting of Prometheus to the rock in accord with the command of Zeus, because he will not tell what the god wants to know. Zeus is determined to force this secret from Prometheus; and Prometheus is equally firm in his resolution to keep it to himself, no matter how keen the torture to which he may be condemned or how prolonged the agony. To Prometheus chained to the crags of the Caucasus other characters come, one after another, some to encourage him in resistance and some to urge him to yield since resistance is ultimately in vain. Altho Zeus does not come the spectators are well aware that it is his unbending volition which is responsible for the situation. Prometheus may vaunt himself to be the master of his fate and captain of his soul; he may steel his will to withstand every outrage; but his invisible opponent has a long arm and a sharp sword in his hand. In the utilization of the device of the unseen duellist, the obvious difference between the 'Death of the Duke of Enghien' and 'Prometheus Bound' lies in the sublety of the later dramatist whereby ne gets his effect without even allowing any of the characters to allege the name of Napoleon, whereas Æschylus causes all his characters to discuss the deeds and the misdeeds of Zeus, and he permits Prometheus to exhale his griefs against the hostile god as often as occasion occurs. There is this further difference also, that M. Hénnique is a sophisticated Parisian who was deliberately achieving his effect by conscious art, whereas Æschylus was a reverent spirit not condescending to artistic subtleties of this sort, even if they had been possible in the primitive conditions of the Attic theater, when tragedies were presented before ten thousand spectators sitting or standing, tier on tier, on the curving hillside of the Acropolis.

(1914.)

IX

SITUATIONS WANTED

I

IN a forgotten book by a forgotten British bard, in the 'Gillot and Goosequill' of Henry S. Leigh, we may read the appealing plaint of a playwright who felt that his invention was failing and who could no longer find the succession of poignant episodes that the drama demands:—

> Ten years I've workt my busy brain
>   In drama for the million;
> I don't aspire to Drury Lane,
>   Nor stoop to the Pavilion.
> I've sought materials low and high
>   To edify the nation;
> At last the fount is running dry—
>   I want a situation.
>
> I've known the day when wicked earls
>   Who made improper offers
> To strictly proper village girls,
>   Could fill a house's coffers.
> The lowly peasant could create
>   A wonderful sensation.
> Such people now are out of date—
>   I want a situation.

The writer of these despondent stanzas had had a hand in a play or two but he was by profession a lyrist and not a dramatist; and it may be doubted whether any of the born playwrights would ever have sent forth this cry of distress, since fecundity is a necessary element in their endowment. The major dramatic poets have always been affluent in their productivity; Sophocles and Shakspere and Molière appear to have averaged two plays in every year of their ripe maturity. It is true, of course, that they had no scruple in taking their material wherever they might find it, not only despoiling their predecessors of single situations, but on occasion helping themselves to a complete plot, ingeniously invented and adroitly constructed and needing only to be transformed and transfigured by their interpreting imagination.

We like to think that in these modern days our dramatists are more conscientious in the acquisition of their raw material, and that they can withstand the temptation to appropriate an entire plot or even a ready-made situation. When Sardou was scientifically interrogated by a physiological psychologist as to his methods of composition he evidently took pleasure in declaring that he had in his notebooks dozens of skeleton stories needing only to be articulated a little more artfully and then to be clothed with words. Probably no one of the playwrights of the second half of the nineteenth century was more fertile in invention than Sardou; and not a few effective situations originally devised by him have been utilized by playmakers in other countries,—one from 'La Haine' for instance in the 'Conquerors' and one from 'La Tosca' in the 'Darling of the Gods.' Notwithstanding this notorious originality Sardou was frequently accused of levying on the inventions of others, without recompense or even acknowledgment; and more than once the accusers caught him "with the goods on him"—if this expressive phrase is permissible. 'Les Pommes du Voisin,' for example, was traced to a story of Charles de Bernard's; 'Fernande' to a tale of Diderot's; and 'Fédora' to a novel of Adolphe Bélot's. As it happened Bélot had dramatized his novel, and when he saw that Sardou had borrowed and bettered his plot, he made no outcry; he contented himself with arranging for a revival of his play, so that the similarity of its story to Sardou's might be made immediately manifest.

When Mario Uchard asserted that the dominant situation in his 'La Fiammina' had been lifted by Sardou for service in 'Georgette,' Sardou retorted by citing three or four earlier pieces and stories in which an identical situation could be found. Those who seek equity must come into court with clean hands; so Uchard lost his case. Nevertheless the impression left upon at

least one reader of the testimony was that Uchard
had no knowledge of the forgotten fictions which
Sardou disinterred, that he believed himself
to be the inventor of the situation in dispute, and
that Sardou probably did derive it from Uchard,
—altho quite possibly he may have invented it
independently.

The fact is indisputable that the number of
situations fit for service on the stage is not in-
finite but rigorously restricted. Gozzi declared
that there were only thirty-six; and when Goethe
and Schiller sought to ascertain these, they could
not fill out the list. Georges Polti accepted
Gozzi's figure and after indefatigable investiga-
tion of several thousand plays, ancient and
modern, he catalogued the three dozen with all
their available corollaries. Of course scientific
certainty is not attainable in such a counting up;
there may be fifty-seven varieties or even ninety
and nine. The playwrights of this generation
have to grind the grist already ground by their
predecessors a generation earlier; they may borrow boldly, that is to say, they may be aware that
what they are doing has been done before, or
they may be innocently original, fondly believing
themselves to be the inventors of a novel predicament and unaware that it was second-hand a
score of centuries before they were born. Their
good faith can not fairly be denied, even if their
originality can be disproved.

There is the Romeo and Juliet situation, for instance,—the course of true love made to run rough by the bitter hostility of the parents. We can find it in 'Huckleberry Finn' in the nineteenth century, and we can also find it in the 'Antigone,' more than two thousand years earlier; and we may rest assured that Mark Twain did not go to Sophocles for it, or even to Shakspere. It is probably to be found in the fiction of every language, dead and alive; and those who employ it now do so without giving a thought to any of its many earlier users. The theme is common property, to be utilized at will by anybody anywhere and anywhen.

II

DURING the run of the 'Chorus Lady' in New York I happened to call the attention of Bronson Howard to the identity of its culminating situation with that in 'Lady Windemere's Fan.' A young woman foolishly adventures herself in the apartment of a man, whereupon an older woman goes there to rescue her; then when the younger woman is summoned to come out of the inner room in which she has taken refuge, it is the older woman who appears, thus placing herself in a compromising position in the eyes of the man whom she is expecting to marry. "Don't forget that I had had it in 'One of Our Girls,'" Howard remarkt, without in any way suggesting that

Oscar Wilde had despoiled him, or that James Forbes had lifted the situation from either of his predecessors. Then I recalled that I had seen it in an unacted play, 'Faith,' by H. C. Bunner, the story of which he had taken as the basis of a novel entitled, 'A Woman of Honor.' Knowing Bunner and Howard intimately, I felt certain that they had no doubt as to their right to utilize this situation, and that if either of them had been conscious of any indebtedness to any specific predecessor he would have declared it frankly.

Bronson Howard, on the playbill of the 'Henrietta,' acknowledged the borrowing of a situation from 'Vanity Fair'; he was compelled to this confession because in this case he happened to know where he had found the situation. He was aware that it was borrowed, and not his own invention. A confession equally complete and of a somewhat larger import is to be found in the Author's Note prefixt to Maeterlinck's play, 'Marie Magdeleine':

"I have borrowed from M. Paul Heyse's drama, 'Maria von Magdala,' the idea of two situations in my play, namely at the end of the first act, the intervention of Christ, who stops the crowd raging against Mary Magdalene, with these words, spoken behind the scenes: 'He that is without sin among you let him cast the first stone'; and in the third the dilemma (in which the great sinner finds herself) of saving or destroying the Son of God, according as she consents or refuses to give herself to a Roman. Before setting to work, I askt the venerable German poet, whom I hold in the highest esteem, for his permission to develop those two situations, which, so to speak, were merely sketcht in his play, with its incomparably richer plot than mine; and offered to recognize his rights in whatever manner he thought proper. My respectful request was answered with a refusal, none too courteous, I regret to say, and almost threatening. From that moment, I was bound to consider that the words from the Gospel quoted above are common property; and that the dilemma of which I speak is one of those which occur pretty frequently in dramatic literature. It seemed to me the more lawful to make use of it inasmuch as I had happened to imagine it in the fourth act of 'Joyzelle' in the same year in which 'Maria von Magdala' was publisht and before I was able to become acquainted with that play."

Then the Belgian poet declared that, except in so far as these two situations were concerned, his play had absolutely nothing in common with the German drama. "Having said this," Maeterlinck concluded, "I am happy to express to the aged master my gratitude for an intellectual benefit, which is not the less great for being involuntary."

This note calls for two comments. The first is that altho the words from the Gospel are common property, still it was Heyse who first applied them to Mary Magdalene; and the second is that altho the dilemma that Maeterlinck wanted to borrow from 'Maria von Magdala' was one that he had already imagined in 'Joyzelle' and one that could be found not infrequently in earlier plays, notably in 'La Tosca' of Sardou, in the 'Dame aux Camélias' of the younger Dumas and in the 'Marion Delorme' of Victor Hugo, still it was Heyse who first had the happy thought of forcing this dilemma upon Mary Magdalene. When the Belgian poet persisted in making his profit out of these two situations of the German story-teller, he may have seemed to some rather high-handed in his forcible rectification of his frontier by the annexation of territory already profitably occupied by his neighbor. To this, it is only fair to answer that the application of the Gospel words and the propounding of this special dilemma to Mary Magdalene were so natural as to be almost necessary, if her story was to be shaped for the stage and sustained by a satisfactory struggle. They are so natural and so necessary that Maeterlinck might almost have been expected to invent them for himself if he had not found them already invented by Heyse.

III

BRONSON HOWARD would have held that Maeterlinck was absolutely within his right in taking over from Herr Heyse what was necessary for the improvement of his own play, if only he declared the indebtedness honestly and if he offered to pay for it. And no playwright was ever more scrupulous in acknowledging his own indebtedness than Howard. The situation which he took from 'Vanity Fair' for use in the 'Henrietta' he might have invented easily enough or he might have found it in half-a-dozen other places besides Thackeray's novel; but as he was aware that it had been suggested to him by Thackeray's novel, he simply had to say so,— just as, many years earlier, on the playbill of his 'Moorcroft,' he had credited the suggestion of its plot to a story by John Hay, altho this source was so remote that Hay was able to say to me that he never would have suspected it except for the note on the program.

When I assert that Howard might easily enough have invented for himself the situation he borrowed from Thackeray I am supported by my own experience. I invented that situation, quite forgetful of the fact that I must once have been familiar with it in 'Vanity Fair'; and I made it the center of a one-act comedy, 'This Picture and That,' written almost simultaneously

with the 'Henrietta.' Only after the performance of my little piece and only when I saw
Howard's play with its note of acknowledgment
to Thackeray, did I feel called upon to doubt
my own originality. A few years thereafter I
had the pleasure and the profit of collaborating
with Howard in the composition of 'Peter Stuy-
vesant, Governor of New Amsterdam,' and when
we were still engaged in the arduous and delightful task of putting together our plot, of setting
our characters upright upon their feet and of
seeking situations in which they might reveal
themselves effectively, I chanced to suggest that
we might perhaps utilize a situation in a certain
French drama. I find that I have now forgotten the situation and the title of the play in
which it appeared. I made the suggestion doubt-
fully, as its acceptance might lay us open to the
accusation of plagiarism.

Howard promptly waved aside my scruples by
a declaration of principle:—"When I am at work
on a play," he explained, "my duty as an artist
is to make that play just as good as I can, to
construct it as perfectly as possible no matter
where I get my materials. If this situation you
suggest is one which will help our play, we should
take it without hesitation. Our scenario is certain to be greatly modified before we are satisfied
with it and ready to begin on the actual writing;
and very likely we shall find that this borrowed

situation which today seems to us helpful will not survive to the final revision; it may have led us to something finer and then itself disappeared. But if, when the play is done at last, we are face to face with the fact that one of our situations came to us from somebody else,—then, our duty as honest men begins. We must give due credit on the playbill when the piece is performed and in the book when it is publisht. Furthermore, if the somebody from whom we have borrowed is alive, if he has rights either legal or moral, we must secure his permission, paying whatever may be necessary."

Bronson Howard was as candid as he was clear-eyed; and the principle he declared is one by which every dramatist would do well to govern himself. If a playwright should be exceedingly scrupulous and seek to avoid the use of any situation invented and utilized by any one of his predecessors in the long history of playmaking, he would soon find himself at a standstill and in a blind alley; he would discover speedily that unused situations are very scarce. The playwright must perforce resign himself to the employment of those which have already seen service. Where there is specific obligation he should acknowledge it frankly,—unless indeed the borrowed situation is so well known that acknowledgment may seem a work of supererogation. It is instantly obvious that the 'Rantzau' of Erck-

mann-Chatrian is an Alsatian 'Romeo and
Juliet' and that the 'André Cornélis' of Paul
Bourget is a Parisian 'Hamlet';—these resemblances were so very evident that they could
not be denied and therefore need not be declared.

IV

WITH characteristic wisdom and with a liberality as characteristic, Goethe held that what was
really important was not where a situation came
from but what use was made of it. He noted
that Scott had helpt himself to a situation from
'Egmont,' and "because he did it well, he deserves praise." We may be sure that Goethe
would have only commendation for the skill with
which the Jacobean playwrights despoiled the
Spanish stage, because these gifted Englishmen
always bettered what they borrowed. In his
illuminating little book on the Spanish drama,
George Henry Lewes called attention to the
imaginative energy with which Fletcher in the
'Custom of the Country,' transformed an ingeniously contrived situation in Calderon's
'Mejor esta que Estaba' into a superbly dramatic scene.

In the Spanish piece, Don Carlos rushes in
and begs Flora to conceal him and save his life.
She has no sooner hidden him than his pur-
suers enter,—to tell her that they have followed

into the house a cavalier who has just killed her
cousin. She keeps her promise to protect the
hidden fugitive; and she tells those who are
seeking him that he sprang from the window into
the garden and so escaped. This is an effective
scene; but it is infinitely inferior to that made
out of it by Fletcher (possibly aided by Mas-
singer). Donna Guiomar is alone in her bed chamber; she is anxious about her absent son and she
kneels in prayer. Rutilio rushes in. He is a
stranger,

> a most unfortunate stranger,
> That, called unto it by my enemy's pride,
> Have left him dead in the streets. Justice pur-
> sues me,
> And for that life I took unwillingly,
> And in a fair defense, I must lose mine,
> Unless you, in your charity, protect me.
> Your house is now my sanctuary!

Donna Guiomar agrees to shelter him and bids
him hide himself in the hangings of her bed,
saying

> Be of comfort;
> Once more I give my promise for your safety.
> All men are subject to such accidents,
> Especially the valiant;—and who knows not,
> But that the charity I afford this stranger,
> My only son elsewhere may stand in need of.

Then enter officers and servants with a bier whereupon a body lies lifeless; and a servant declares that

> Your only son,
> My lord Duarte's slain!

And an officer explains that

> his murderer,
> Pursued by us, was by a boy discovered
> Entering your house.

The noble mother, stricken to the heart, is true to her promise. She tells the officers to go forth and search for the murderer. Then at last when she is left alone with the corpse of her son, she orders the concealed slayer to make his escape:—

> Come fearless forth! But let thy face be cover'd,
> That I hereafter be not forc'd to know thee!

This is an incomparable example of the deep difference between the theatrically effective and the truly dramatic,—between adroit story-telling on the stage for the sake of the story itself, and story-telling for the sake of the characters involved in the situation. The incident invented by Calderon is ingenious and it provides a shock of surprise and a thrill of suspense; but how much richer and nobler is the situation as Fletcher improved it, and how superbly did he phrase the motive and the emotion of the stricken mother! The Jacobean poet achieved surprise and suspense and also a larger significance, because he had imagination to project the scene as a whole, to prepare it, to express its ultimate value, and to end it to the keen satisfaction of the spectators.

v

THE younger Dumas, a playmaker of surprising skill, was once persuaded to rewrite a play by Émile de Girardin, the 'Supplice d'une Femme.' The original author protested that he could not recognize his drama in the new version. Dumas explained that the original play had been cast aside because it was a poor piece of work, quite impossible on the stage. But it had a central situation which Dumas declared to be very interesting and very dramatic; and therefore Dumas had written a new play to present this novel and powerful situation so as to make it effective in the theater, which was precisely what Girardin had been incapable of doing, altho he had himself invented the situation.

"But a situation is not an idea," Dumas explained in the article in which he justified his rejection of Girardin's plot and construction.

177

"An idea has a beginning, a middle and an end, —an exposition, a development and a conclusion. Anybody may happen on a dramatic situation; but it must be prepared for; it must be made possible and acceptable; and above all the knot must be untied logically." Then Dumas illustrated these assertions by suggesting the kind of dramatic situation which anybody might happen on. A young man falls in love with a girl; he asks her hand; and they are married. Then, and only then, at the very moment when he is about to bear her away to their future home, he learns categorically that he has married his own sister. "There's a situation! and very interesting indeed. But how are you going to get out of it? I give you a thousand guesses—and then I give you the situation itself, if you want it. He who can start with this and make a good play out of it, will be the real author of that play, and I shall claim no share in it."

The situation, around which Girardin had written the 'Supplice d'une Femme,' was difficult and it was dangerous; but it was not impossible. Dumas was able to find a way out and to bestow upon the story an attractive exposition, a highly emotional development and a conclusion at once logical and acceptable to a profitable succession of audiences. And this is just what one of the establisht American dramatists was able to do recently for a novice who had happened on a strong and striking situation. The piece in which the 'prentice playwright had put his situation was promptly rejected by all the managers, until at last in despair he went to the older dramatist for advice. He had put his powerful situation in the first act, so that it was inadequately prepared for while its superior weight prevented his giving to the later acts the increasing force which later acts ought to possess. The remedy suggested by the more experienced dramatist was simple; it was to begin and to end the story earlier— to cancel the original second and third acts, and to compose a new first and second act to lead up to the strong and striking situation, which could then be amply developt in the new third and last act to be made out of the material in the original first act.

VI

In 'Rupert of Hentzau,' the sequel to the 'Prisoner of Zenda,' there is a superb situation which needed to be solved and which cried aloud for poetic treatment. Rudolph Rassendyll looks almost exactly like the King of Ruritania. In the 'Prisoner of Zenda' circumstances force him to take the King's place and to be crowned in his stead; so it is that he meets the King's cousin, the Princess Flavia, and falls in love with her and she with· him. In 'Rupert of Hentzau' we find that the Princess for reasons of state has

179

married her cousin; and then circumstances again force Rassendyll to personate the King, who is suddenly murdered and his body burnt. What is Rassendyll to do? Shall he accept the throne and take with it the Queen who loves him and whom he loves? The Queen begs him to do this for her sake. If he decides to profit by this series of accidents, then he must, for the rest of his life, live a lie, knowing that he is holding that to which he has no right, legal or moral.

Here is the stuff out of which serious drama is made; here is one of the great passionate crises of existence, when, in Stevenson's phrase, "duty and inclination come nobly to the grapple." Here is an ethical dilemma demanding a large and lofty poetic treatment,—like that which Fletcher bestowed on the situation he borrowed from Calderon. Unfortunately the author of the story was unable to rise to this exalted altitude; and he got out of the complication by a tame device, which simply dodged the difficulty. Before the hero can declare his decision, he is assassinated. The author had happened on a fine situation; he was adroit in his exposition of it and in his development; but he failed to find a fit conclusion.

Perhaps, in the course of time, when the hour strikes for a rebirth of the poetic drama, a dramatist of a later generation,—a poet who is truly a playwright and a playwright who is really a poet,—will be tempted to take over this situation invented by the ingenious novelist; and he may be able to discover a satisfactory conclusion and to treat it with the interpreting imagination it demands.

(1917.)

X

THE PLAYWRIGHT AND THE PLAYER

I

IN one of his essays Robert Louis Stevenson
discust the technic of style; and he felt it
necessary to begin by apologizing and by admitting that to the average man there is nothing
more disenchanting "than to be shown the springs
and mechanism of any art. All our arts and occu-
pations lie wholly on the surface; it is on the
surface that we perceive their beauty, fitness,
and significance; and to pry below is to be
appalled by their emptiness and shockt by the
coarseness of the strings and pulleys." He insisted that most of us dislike all explanations of
artistic method, on the principle laid down in
'Hudibras':—

Still the less they understand
The more they admire the sleight-of-hand.

No doubt, this is true of the majority, who are
delighted by the result of the conjuror's skill and
prefer not to have its secret revealed to them.
But it is not true of a minority who are ever

eager to discover the devices whereby the marvel has been wrought; and it is this minority who constitute the insiders, so to speak, so far as that art is concerned, the majority being content to be forever outsiders ignorant of the technical difficulties and the technical dangers which the artist has triumphantly overcome. The insider, the expert, the artist himself, the critic of wise penetration, is ever intensely interested in technic,— as Stevenson himself testified in another essay: "A technicality is always welcome to the expert, whether in athletics, art or law; I have heard the best kind of talk on technicalities from such rare and happy persons as both know and love their business."

It is a sign of the constantly increasing interest in the drama that more and more theatergoers are showing an eager desire to understand the secrets of the two allied arts of the theater,— the art of the playmaker and the art of the player, each dependent upon the other, each incapable of exercise without the aid of the other. The work of the author can be revealed completely only by the work of the actor; and the actor can do nothing unless the author gives him something to do. The dramaturgic art and the histrionic art are interdependent; they are Siamese twins, bound by a tie of flesh and blood. They can quarrel, as perhaps Chang and Eng may have had their fraternal disagreements; but they can separate only under the penalty of a double death. At every hour of their joint existence they have to consider and to serve one another, whatever their jealousies may be.

It is true that there have been periods when acting flourisht and the drama languisht, as in the midyears of the nineteenth century in Great Britain and the United States. Yet in these decades the performer unprovided with profitable parts by the playwrights of his own time, was able to find what he needed in the plays of the past, in which moreover he could experience the keen pleasure of measuring himself with the memory of the foremost performers of the preceding generation. John Philip Kemble cared little for new parts in new plays; and it was said of him that he thought all the good parts had already been written. Edwin Booth was content with the characters that Shakspere had created; and Joseph Jefferson found in one of Sheridan's comedies a character he preferred to any of those in the countless modern plays which aspiring authors were forever pestering him to produce.

It needs to be noted however that there is danger to the drama in these periods when the actor is supreme and when he feels at liberty to revise the masterpieces of the past in accord with his own whim and perhaps in compliance with his own self-esteem. Jefferson was both skilful and tactful in his rearrangement of the

'Rivals'; he added but little of his own and what he omitted was little loss. None the less was there a certain justice in the gibe of his cousin, William Warren, to the effect that however delightful Jefferson's Bob Acres might be, it left "Sheridan twenty miles away." Far less excusable was Macready's violent condensation of the 'Merchant of Venice' into a mere Shylock piece, omitting the final act at Belmont and ending with the trial scene.

It is in these periods of dramatic penury that the actor is able to usurp an undue share of popular attention. In periods of dramatic productivity his importance is less unduly magnified; and even if plays are written specially for him, they are rarely mere vehicles for the display of his histrionic accomplishment; most of them are solidly constructed works of art, in which the character he is to personate is kept in its proper proportion to the others. A playwright willing to manufacture a piece which is only a vehicle for an actor is humbling himself to be the domestic of the practitioner of the sister art. But the dramatist who is not eager to profit by the special gifts of the foremost actors, who are his contemporaries and his comrades, is simply neglecting his obvious opportunities.

II

IT is a credit and not a discredit to Sophocles and to Shakspere, to Molière and to Racine, to Sheridan and to Augier that they made use of the possibilities they perceived in the performers of their own time. It may be a discredit to Sardou that he wrote a series of effective but false melodramas for Sarah-Bernhardt, not because he composed these plays for her, but because they were unworthy of him. It was not a discredit to Rostand that he put together 'Cyrano de Bergerac' and 'L'Aiglon' and 'Chantecler,' one after another, in order that the dominant character in each should be impersonated by the incomparably versatile Coquelin, because in composing them for this comedian the author did not subordinate himself; because he did not sacrifice a play to a part; and because he was not content, as Sardou had been, to make a whole play out of a single part.

To those who had followed the career of this comedian it was obvious that 'Cyrano de Bergerac' had been written not only for Coquelin but around him, in order to let him display in one piece as many as possible of the facets of his genius already disclosed in a host of other plays. It was equally evident that 'Chantecler,' with all its lyric exuberance, was also a play tailor-made for the brilliant comedian with the clarion voice, who could be both vivacious and pathetic. It is even possible that the first suggestion of this barnyard fantasy may be found in the fact that the comedian was in the habit of signing his notes to his intimates with the single syllable "Coq."

But it is likely to surprize those who remember that the part of the 'Eaglet' was written for Sarah-Bernhardt and that Coquelin did not appear in the play when it was originally performed, to learn that none the less was it begun with the sole intention of providing him with a congenial character. Yet such is the case, as Coquelin told me himself.

As he and Rostand were leaving one of the final rehearsals of 'Cyrano,' the poet said to the player, "this is not going to be the last piece that I shall write for you, of course. Tell me now, what kind of a character do you want?"

And Coquelin answered politely that he would be delighted to produce any piece that Rostand might bring him.

"No, no," returned the author; "that is all very well; but what I'd like to do is to write a play specifically for you, and to please you. Isn't there some character which you have always longed to impersonate and which has never come your way?"

Coquelin thought for a moment and then he admitted that there was one type which he had not attempted and which he had often wisht to act. This was an aging veteran of Napoleon's armies, who had followed the Little Corporal in all his campaigns from Egypt to Russia,—the type depicted in Raffet's sketches, the type familiarly known as "the old grumbler of the Empire," *le vieux grognard de l'Empire*.

"Excellent!" cried Rostand. "Excellent! I shall set to work on it as soon as we get 'Cyrano' out of the way."

If this was the starting point of 'L'Aiglon,' how was it that the play was written for Sarah-Bernhardt and not for Coquelin? And to find the answer to this we must go into the workshop of the dramatist. If the old soldier of Napoleon is to be the central figure of the play, then Napoleon himself must not appear in the piece, since the Emperor was a personality so overmastering that he could not be made a subordinate in the story. Therefore the action must take place after Napoleon's exile and death. Yet, after all, the old soldier is devoted to Napoleon; and if he is to be interesting on the stage, he must be a man of action, strong-willed, resolute and ingenious; he must be engaged in a plot intimately related to Napoleon. It is well known that after the return of the Bourbons the Bonapartists were speedily disaffected and that there were several intrigues to restore the empire with Napoleon's son as Emperor.

Thus Rostand was led irresistibly to the little

King of Rome, an exile in Austria living almost in captivity with his Austrian mother. And then all the possibilities of the pale and pathetic profile of the Eaglet disclosed themselves to Rostand one after another; and from the old soldier planning to put his master's son on his master's throne the poet's interest shifted to the young prince, in whom there were resemblances to 'Richard II' and to 'Hamlet.' So the Duke of Reichstadt became the hero of the piece and took the center of the stage. Yet the old soldier Flambeau still occupied Rostand's mind and he was allowed to occupy a wholly disproportionate space in the play. In the plot of 'L'Aiglon' as it was finally elaborated, Flambeau ought to have been only one of a host of accessory characters revolving around the feeble and weak-willed prince crusht beneath a responsibility far beyond his capacity.

III

WHEN Jules Lemaitre, as the critic of the *Débats*, was called on to comment upon his own comedy, 'L'Age Difficile,' he contented himself with telling his readers how he came to write the play and with describing the successive steps of its inception, growth, and composition. The exciting cause was the suggestion that he should prepare a piece for Coquelin. Naturally he was delighted at the possibility of having so accom-

plisht an interpreter for the chief character of the
play he might write; and his invention was instantly set in motion.   As an actor is likely to be
most effective when he is least made up, Lemaitre
started with Coquelin as a man of about forty-
five or fifty; and this led him to consider the
special dangers of that period in a man's life.
So it was that he hit upon the theme of his
comedy, the 'Difficult Age'; and this theme he
developt so richly that the story seemed to have
been devised solely to illustrate the thesis.   In
fact, if Lemaitre had not frankly confest that the
exciting cause of his comedy was the desire to
find a part to fit Coquelin, no spectator of the
play would ever have suspected it.

If there had been no Coquelin, there would
have been no 'Age Difficile' and no 'Chantecler,'
no 'Aiglon' and no 'Cyrano de Bergerac,'—just
as it is possible that without Mlle. Champsmeslé
there might have been no 'Phèdre' and without
Burbage there might have been no 'Hamlet,' no
'Othello' and no 'Lear.'   For the full expansion of
the energy of the dramatic poet the stimulus of
the actor is as necessary as the response of the
audience.   In his old age Goethe confided to
Eckermann that he had been discouraged as a
dramatist by the lack of these two necessities.
" If I had produced an effect, and had met with
applause, I would have written a round dozen of
pieces such as 'Iphigenia' and 'Tasso': there was

no deficiency of material. But actors were wanting to represent such pieces with life and spirit; and a public was wanting to hear and receive them with sympathy."

The merely literary critic who judges a drama as if it were a lyric, as if it were simply the expression of the poet's mood at the moment of creation, often fails to understand the play because he has no consciousness of the complexity of the dramatic art, which must needs languish unless there is the hearty coöperation of the three necessary elements,—the playwright to compose, the player to impersonate, and the playgoer to respond to the double appeal of player and playwright.

The dramatists have always been conscious of the intimacy with which their work is associated with the work of the actors. In the preface to one of his slightest pieces, 'L'Amour Médecin,' Molière put his opinion on record: "Everybody knows that comedies are written only to be acted, and I recommend the reading of this play only to those who have eyes to discover while reading all the by-play of the stage." And Mr. Henry Arthur Jones asserts that "actors are on the stage to fill in a hundred supplementary touches to the author's ten;—but this leads to the quaintest results, since the actor has the choice of filling in the wrong hundred in the wrong places. And the public and critics always suppose that he has filled them in rightly. How can they do otherwise? They can judge only by what they see and hear."

IV

HERE is what may be called the paradox of dramatic criticism—that on the first night of an unpublisht play, the public and the critics have to take the performance as a whole, finding it a task of insuperable delicacy to disentangle the work of the players from the work of the playwright. They can form their opinion of the value of the play itself only from that single performance; and they can form their opinion of the value of the individual actor only from the impression he has made at that performance. Now, it is matter of common knowledge that sometimes good parts are ill-played and bad parts well-played. But on the first night, how are the public and the critics to know in advance which are the good parts and which are the bad parts? There are parts which seem to be showy and effective, and which are not so in reality. In French there is a term for them;—"false good parts," *faux bons rôles*. For example, in Sardou's 'Patrie,' perhaps his finest play, the heroine has to express an incessant series of emotions; she has abundant occasion for powerful acting; and yet half-a-dozen actresses of authority have been tempted to essay the part without success. The character is high-strung and wilful, but she is not true and sincere; she is artificial and arbitrary; and the audience is dumbly conscious of this trickiness and looks on at her exhibition of histrionics with languid sympathy. It is a false good part.

On the other hand there are parts that "play themselves" and there are pieces that are "actor-proof"—effective even if performed only by an ordinary company without any actors of accredited ability. Hamlet is a part that "plays itself," since the plot of the piece is so moving that it supports the performer of the central figure even if he is not really equal to the character. George Henry Lewes asserted that no one of the leading English tragedians had ever completely failed as Hamlet,—whereas the greatest of them all, David Garrick, had made so complete a fiasco as Othello that he never dared to appear in the piece a second time.

The 'Tartuffe' of Molière is an actor-proof play, holding the interest of the audience even when an uninspired company is giving a ragged performance. Almost as actor-proof are 'As You Like It' and the 'School for Scandal.' All three of these comedies reward the most competent and the most careful performance; but they do not demand this. Their appeal is so broad and so certain that they can be carried off by good will, aided in the case of the two English comedies by high spirits. Then too their reputation is solidly establisht and widespread; and the spectator comes to them assured that he will have entertainment, predisposed to easy enjoyment. Quite possibly no one of the three comedies was actor-proof at its first performance; and perhaps they might then have been killed by an inadequate performance of any one of their more important characters.

Molière was his own stage-manager and at the first performance of 'L'Amour Médecin' he was responsible for "all the by-play of the stage." And when Mr. Henry Arthur Jones produces his own plays he takes care that the actor shall not fill in the wrong "hundred supplementary touches." But when the author of the play is dead or unable to be present at the rehearsals, we sometimes see "the quaintest results." There are actors who are supersubtle in the supplying of the little touches which the dramatist has left to their discretion, and who so embroider the parts they are playing that the main outline is obscured and enfeebled.

At the end of the nineteenth century there was an actor of prominence whose career I had followed with interest for more than a score of years, observing the expansion of his reputation and the deterioration of his art. When I first saw him on the stage he was direct and swift, creating a character in bold outline; and at the end of a quarter of a century he had become painfully over-ingenious in the accumulation of superfluities of detail which maskt the main lines of the part. In fact he had begun by acting inside the character and he had ended by acting outside it. The result was quaint enough; but it was also pitiably ineffective; and if the authors of the plays he thus disfigured by the trivialities of his jig-saw fret-work could have beheld his performance, they would have cried out in protest at this betrayal of their purpose.

(1915.)

XI

IRISH PLAYS AND IRISH PLAYWRIGHTS

I

IT is one of the many interesting and significant coincidences of history that the more completely a smaller country may be absorbed into a larger nation, the more likely are the inhabitants of the lesser community to cherish their own provincial peculiarities. They seek to keep alive the local traditions and to revive the local customs; and often they strive to reinvigorate the local dialect and to raise it to a loftier level, that it may be fitter to express their local patriotism, different from their larger national patriotism but in no wise antagonistic to it. As a result of this pride in the past and of this pleasure in the present there is likely to arise a local literature in the local variation from the standard speech of the nation—the standard speech assiduously taught in the schools, which are ever struggling to eradicate in the illiterate every vestige of the dialect that the men of letters are cultivating with careful art. And this deliberate provincialism is not factional or separatist; it indicates no relaxing of loyalty toward the nation. Indeed, in so far as any political significance is concerned, the outflowering of a dialect literature may be taken as evidence of national solidarity and of the dying down of older sectional animosities.

It was in the last quarter of the eighteenth century and in the first quarter of the nineteenth, when Scotland had at last accepted the Hanoverian succession, that Burns and Scott and lesser lyrists of a varying endowment made use of the broad Scots tongue to sing the sorrows and the joys of the North Briton. It was in the third and fourth quarter of the nineteenth century, after the fierce ardor of the Revolutionary expansion and of the Napoleonic conquests had finally welded France into a self-conscious unity, that Mistral and his fellow-bards told again the old legends of Provence and illumined that fair land with new tales of no less charm, all composed in a modern revision of the soft and gentle speech of the troubadours. And now it is just at the beginning of the twentieth century, after three score years of incessant agitation have removed most of the wrongs of the Irish people, that Yeats and Synge and Lady Gregory have bidden their fellow-countrymen to gaze at themselves in the mirror of the drama and to listen to their own persuasive brogue.

Surprize has been exprest at the sudden burgeoning forth of this new Irish drama almost at the behest of Lady Gregory. But when due consideration is given to the long list of Irishmen who have held their own in the English theater, there is cause for wonder rather that Ireland did not have a drama of its own long ago. In fact the history of English dramatic literature, and more especially the record of English comedy, would be sadly shrunken if the Hibernian contribution could be cancelled. We can estimate the gap that this operation would make when we recall the names of George Farquhar, Richard Steele, Oliver Goldsmith, Richard Brinsley Sheridan, John O'Keefe, Sheridan Knowles, Samuel Lover, Dion Boucicault, John Brougham, Oscar Wilde, Bernard Shaw and "George A. Birmingham." There is food for thought as well as for laughter in the saying that "English comedy has either been written by Irishmen or else adapted from the French." A harsh and cynical critic might even go further and add—having Steele in mind for one and for another Boucicault— that sometimes English comedy has been both written by an Irishman and adapted from the French.

It is to English comedy that these Irishmen contributed; it is not to Irish comedy. The admission may be made that one or another of them now and again sketcht a fellow-countryman or two; but before Lover and Boucicault no one of these Irish dramatists peopled a play with Irish characters and laid its scene in Ireland.

Altho they must have known Ireland and the Irish better than they knew England and the English, it is to the portrayal of the latter that they gave their loving attention, neglecting altogether the delineation of the former. For some reason they were not tempted to employ their talents at home and to devote themselves to the depicting of the manners and customs of their own island. Probably the explanation of their refusal to utilize the virgin material that lay ready to their hands is to be found in the fact that to achieve a living wage they had to write for the London theaters, the audiences of which took little or no interest either in Ireland or in the Irish.

Whatever the reason may be why these brilliant Irish playwrights did not write plays of Irish life, there is no denying that they did not, and that it was left for the contemporary supporters of the Abbey Theater to plow the fresh fields which their predecessors had refused to cultivate. Even the later English comic dramatists of Irish birth have eschewed themes fundamentally Irish and have rarely introduced Irish characters into their English plays; there is not a single Irish part in all Oscar Wilde's comedies and there is only one of Mr. Shaw's pieces the scene of which is laid in Ireland. Irish novelists, Maria Edgeworth, Banin, Carleton, Lever and Lover, won fame by writing Irish stories; but only Lover and

Boucicault wrote Irish plays. The Irish dramatists were all of them working for the London market and they were subdued to what they workt in.

II

WHEN we consider the closeness of Ireland to England, and the ease of communication we can only marvel at the infrequency with which Irish characters appear in English plays. There is no Irishman—except the slim profile of Captain Macmorris in 'Henry V'—in all Shakspere's comedies and histories and tragedies, altho there are Scotsmen and Welshmen. Apparently the earliest Irish character in the English drama did not step on the stage until after the Restoration and nearly fifty years after Shakspere's death. This earliest Irish character was a comic servant, called Teague, who appears in Sir Robert Howard's 'Committee,' a play which Pepys went to see in June, 1663. And apparently the second Irish character was another Tegue in Shadwell's 'Lancashire Witches and Tegue O'Divelly the Irish Priest,' a highly colored piece which was produced in 1681. The first Teague was devised to provoke laughter, whereas the second Tegue was intended to be detested and despised as an intriguing villain. It seems probable that this portrayal of a Hibernian scoundrel by an English playwright was pleasing to the London playgoers, since Shadwell brought him forward again a few years later in another play, the 'Amorous Bigot,' produced in 1690.

Then came the first of the native Irishmen who were to brighten English comedy with their ingenuity and their wit, and their grace and their good humor—the first, and perhaps the most gifted of them all, George Farquhar. After trying his wings in public as an actor, an experience which explains the superior briskness and theatrical effectiveness of his plays over those of his immediate predecessors, Congreve, Wycherly and Vanbrugh, he went over to London and "commenced playwright." Yet he did not draw on his knowledge of his own people; and in all his plays we find only two relatively unimportant and absolutely insignificant Irish characters. One of these is another Teague in the more or less successful 'Twin Rivals,' produced in 1705; and the other is an Irish priest in the triumphantly successful 'Beaux' Stratagem,' produced in 1707.

We cannot even guess what Farquhar might have done if he had survived, and whether or not he would have drawn more richly upon his recollections of his fellow-countrymen after his repeated success had given him confidence in himself and authority over the public. His career was cut short by death before he was thirty—about the age when Sheridan abandoned playmaking for politics. It has been noted that the novelist is likely to flower late and often not fully to reveal his capacity as a creator of character until he is forty, whereas the dramatist may win his spurs when he is still in the first flush of youth. Playmaking demands inventive cleverness, first of all, and dexterity of craftsmanship, and these are qualities which a young man may possess in abundance almost as native gifts, even tho he may not have had time to reflect deeply upon the spectacle of human folly, which is the prime staple of comedy.

It is possibly because he was an Irishman that Farquhar's morality is not ignoble like Congreve's and Wycherly's. He is not to be classed with the rest of the Restoration dramatists, as is usually done. Farquhar may offend our latterday propriety, now and again, by his plain-spoken speech, but he is never foul in his plotting, as are Wycherly and Congreve, whom he surpasses also in the adroitness of this plotting. His dialog can be clensed by excision, whereas their dirt lies deeper and cannot be overcome by all the perfumes of Araby. It is upon Farquhar that Sheridan modelled himself, and not upon Congreve as has often been assumed. The 'School for Scandal' may reveal an attempt to echo the wit of the 'Way of the World'; but its solid structure and its skilful articulation of incident disclose a close study of the 'Inconstant,' the 'Recruiting Officer' and the 'Beaux' Stratagem,' all of them frequently acted when Sheridan was serving his apprenticeship as a playwright.

III

IN crediting Farquhar with a finer moral sense than Congreve or Wycherly, it must in fairness be noted that they composed their more important comedies before Jeremy Collier had attackt the rampant indecency which characterized the English comic drama at the end of the seventeenth century, and that Farquhar came forward as a playwright after the non-conformist divine had cleared the air by his bugle-blast. The dramatist who took Collier's remarks most to heart was Farquhar's contemporary and fellow Irishman, Steele. But unlike Farquhar, Steele decided to be deliberately didactic. He declared that in his comedy, the 'Funeral,' produced in 1701, altho it was "full of incidents that move laughter," nevertheless "virtue and vice appear just as they ought to do." Steele was even more ostentatiously moral in the 'Lying Lover,' produced in 1704 and withdrawn ofter only a few performances, its author asserting sadly that the play had been "damned for its piety." Yet in neither of these early comedies, nor later in the 'Conscious Lovers,' does Steele introduce any Irish character.

And we do not discover any Irish character in

either of the comedies of Oliver Goldsmith, the 'Good-natured Man,' produced in 1768, and 'She Stoops to Conquer,' produced in 1773. A year after this second comedy had establisht itself as a favorite on the stage, where it is still seen with pleasure after seven score years, Goldsmith died, at the comparatively early age of forty-six. Here again, it is idle to speculate on what he might have achieved as a dramatist after the stage-doors had swung wide to welcome him. If he had survived, it is possible that he might have been tempted to take a theme from his native island and to treat it with all his genial insight into human nature, never likely to be keener or more caressing than in dealing with his own countrymen.

Two years after Goldsmith had brought out 'She Stoops to Conquer,' Sheridan brought out the 'Rivals,' to be followed in swift succession and with equal success by the 'Duenna,' the 'School for Scandal' and the 'Critic.' Then he forsook the theater for the more temporary stage offered to him by politics. In only one of these varied masterpieces of comedy is there an Irish character. This single specimen is Sir Lucius O'Trigger in the 'Rivals,' easily the best Irish part that had yet appeared in any comedy, and surpast by scarcely any Irish character in any later play, English or Irish. Sir Lucius is an Irish gentleman; he is essentially a gentleman and he is intensely Irish. Here was a novelty, since most of the few Irish characters already introduced into English comedy had been servants, first of all, and secondly only superficially Irish. Oddly enough, the bad acting of the original impersonator of Sir Lucius, a performer named Lee, almost caused the failure of the 'Rivals' at the first and second performances. The comedy was then withdrawn for repairs, and for the rehearsal of another actor, Clinch, as Sir Lucius. In gratitude to Clinch for the rescue of the 'Rivals' from the doom that impended, Sheridan improvised for his benefit a two-act farce, called 'St. Patrick's Day, or the Scheming Lieutenant,' a lively little play of no importance, in which Clinch appeared as the scheming lieutenant, an Irishman, only superficially Hibernian.

It is strange that the popularity of Sir Lucius and his appeal to the public did not lure the later English comic dramatists of Irish nativity to invite other characters over from the island of their own birth. But we do not recall any Irish part in any of the many plays of John O'Keefe, only one of whose comedies 'Wild Oats' is ever seen on the stage of today, and then only at intervals which are constantly lengthening. Nor can we recall any Irish part in any of the toplofty comedies of Sheridan Knowles, composed partly in turgid prose and partly in very blank verse, devoid all of them of the wit and the gaiety and the liveliness which we believe we have a right to expect from an Irish dramatist.

Very Irish however are the pieces made out of the 'Handy Andy' and the 'Rory O'Moore' of Samuel Lover; and most characteristically Hibernian is the lighthearted hero of Lover's farcical little fantasy called the 'Happy Man.' That these slight plays of Lover's represent almost the only attempts to deal with Irish character on the English stage in the earlier half of the nineteenth century is the more surprizing since Miss Edgeworth had long since disclosed the richness of the material proffering itself to any keen observer intimate with Irish conditions. Walter Scott, at least, had seen the value of 'Castle Rackrent' and of the 'Absentee'; and he is on record as confessing that one of the motives which urged him to the composition of 'Waverly,' and of its immediate successors, was the desire to do for the Scottish peasant what Miss Edgeworth had done for the Irish peasant. It is to be regretted that the most popular of the Irish followers of Scott in the writing of tales of adventure was Charles Lever, whose earlier and more rollicking romances are happy-go-lucky in their plotting, and never disclose any desire for significant character-delineation. Lever's scampering stories were so loose-jointed that they were almost impossible to dramatize, and even when they were turned into plays they did not demand critical consideration.

IV

THEN toward the end of the first half of the nineteenth century appeared the most prolific of all native Irish playwrights, Dion Boucicault. But it was long after he had become a very expert purveyor of theatrical wares for the theaters of London and New York that Boucicault turned to his native island for a theme. His first play was 'London Assurance,' a five-act comedy with its scene laid in England and with a single Irish character. There is a green-room tradition that the play had been put together by another young and aspiring Irishman, John Brougham, that its original title was 'Irish Assurance,' and that the part now called Dazzle had originally borne an Irish name, having been intended by the ambitious Brougham for his own acting. Nearly forty years ago, when I ventured to ask Brougham as to this tradition and as to his share in the composition of the play, he laughed a little sadly, and then gave me this enigmatic answer, "Well, I've been paid not to claim it!"

Whatever may have been Brougham's share in the beginning, there can be no dispute as to Boucicault's share at the end. 'London Assurance' is not like 'Playing with Fire' or any other of Brougham's later plays; and it is exactly like 'Old Heads and Young Hearts' and half-a-dozen of Boucicault's succeeding comedies, the work all of them of an old heart and a young head,—hard, glittering, insincere and theatrically effective. In these pieces Boucicault was compounding five-act comedies in accord with the traditional formula of the English stage, inherited from Sheridan and Congreve, and becoming at every remove more remote from reality and more resolutely artificial. Altho one of this early group of Boucicault's comedies was called the 'Irish Heiress,' they were all English plays, with only a rare Irish character. A few years later, after Boucicault had become an actor himself, he wrote for his own acting a series of pleasantly sentimental Irish melodramas stuft with sensational scenery,— 'Arrah-na-Pogue' with its sinking wall, the 'Shaughraun' with its turning tower, and the 'Colleen Bawn' with the spectacular dive of its hero into the pool where its heroine is drowning. The theatrical effectiveness of these pieces was undeniable and it was rewarded by long continued popular approval; but no one of them had any validity as a study of life and character in Ireland. They were very clever indeed, but they were only clever; and they but skimmed the surface of life, never cutting beneath it to lay bare unexpected aspects of human nature. It is characteristic that two of the later pieces in which Boucicault appeared as an Irishman were adaptations from the French, 'Daddy O'Dowd' (from 'Les Crochets du Père Martin') and

'Kerry' (from 'La Joie fait Peur'). That he could so twist these French plots with their foreign motives as to make them masquerade as Irish plays is testimony to his incessant cleverness; but it is evidence also that the Irish veneer was so thin as to be almost transparent.

Yet however artificial and superficial might be these Irish pieces of Boucicault's, at least they were more or less Irish, in that they pretended to deal with Irish life in Ireland itself. This is what no one of the earlier Irishmen writing plays for the London stage had ventured to attempt; and it was what the wittiest Irish dramatist of the generation following Boucicault's never did. Oscar Wilde was an Irishman who never toucht an Irish theme or sketcht an Irish character. He never put into his plays any of the haunting sadness, the humorous melancholy of Ireland. He was not quite as free-handed as Boucicault in levying on the private property of his contemporaries, yet he was willing enough to take his own wherever he found it. His dramatic methods are derivative, to put it mildly. Altho he composed a 'Duchess of Padua' more or less in imitation of Victor Hugo and a 'Salome' more or less in imitation of Flaubert, the most popular of his plays are comedies of modern London life, more or less in imitation of Sardou. 'Lady Windemere's Fan' is in accord with the latest Parisian fashion of the season in which it was originally

produced; and even the young girl's trick of uttering only the same two words,—"Yes, mamma"—
in answer to all questions is an echo of Gondinet's
'Oh, Monsieur.' The more farcical comedy called
the 'Importance of being Earnest' is a striking
example of Wilde's imitative method, the first
act and half of the second act having a closely
knit comic embroglio such as we find in Labiche's
'Plus Heureux des Trois' and 'Célimare le Bien-
Aimé' and the rest of the piece being loosely
put together in the whimsical manner of W. S.
Gilbert's 'Engaged.'

There is nothing in any of Oscar Wilde's plays
to reveal his Irish birth—unless we may credit
to his nativity his abundant cleverness and his
ready wit, the coruscating fireworks of which
were sometimes exploded by an ill-concealed
slow-match. It is almost as tho the apostle of
estheticism recoiled from his native island and
deliberately refused to be interested in his
fellow-countrymen. And almost the same remark might be made about a later and far more
richly gifted English author of Irish birth,
Bernard Shaw. Of all his score or more plays
only one, 'John Bull's Other Island' is Irish in
its subject; and this sole exception, so the author
himself tells us, was due to the urgent request
of Yeats, who begged him to come to the aid
of the struggling Abbey Theater in Dublin. As
it happens, 'John Bull's Other Island' was never

produced at the playhouse for which it was composed, because, as Shaw confesses, "it was un-
congenial to the whole spirit of the neo-Gaelic
movement, which is bent on creating a new
Ireland after its own ideal."

V

In the United States, with our scattered Irish
contingent, Boucicault's Irish pieces were as
successful as they were in Great Britain. John
Brougham, following in Boucicault's footsteps,
wrote plays to order for Barney Williams and
William J. Florence, cutting his cloth close to the
figure of the special performer he was fitting. In
the American variety-shows a host of Irish im-
personators of both sexes presented broad caricatures of Irish character often rooted in reality.
And here in New York there was develop out
of these variety-show caricatures a special type
of robust Irish comedy, more veracious than Boucicault's sentimental melodramas. Edward Harrigan began with a mere sketch, the·'Mulligan
Guards,' peopled with half-a-dozen species of
Irishmen acclimated in America; and as he was
encouraged by immediate appreciation on the
part of our cosmopolitan and hospitable public,
he went on, feeling his way and refining his
method, until he attained the summit of his reach
in the delightful 'Squatter Sovereignty,' with its

beautifully differentiated groups of the clan Murphy and the clan Macintyre. It need not be denied that there were wilful extravagances in this series of studies of the New York Irishman and that to the very end there were traces of the variety-show out of which this type of play had been evolved; but no native Irishman had a more realistic humor than Harrigan nor a keener insight into human nature.

Then we come to the beginning of the twentieth century and to the founding of the Abbey Theater in Dublin, to the movement led by Lady Gregory and adorned by the widely different talents of Yeats and Synge. Here was at last a new departure of the Irish drama in Ireland itself. Here were plays of very varying value and of many different kinds, alike only in this, that they eschewed manufactured bulls; that they did not rely on a varnish of paraded brogue; that they did not deal in boisterous fun-making for its own sake,—their fun depending rather upon a subtler humor tinged with melancholy; and that they were no longer contented with an external indication of superficial Irish characteristics, but sought an internal and intimate expression of the essential. These new Irish plays were not Irish by accident; they were Irish by intention, Irish in character and in action, Irish in motive and in sentiment, Irish thru and thru, immitigably Irish.

The late Laurence Hutton once defined an American play as a play written by an American on an American theme and carried on solely by American characters; but he had to confess the falsity of this definition when it was pointed out to him that so rigid a demand would exclude from the French drama the 'Cid' of Corneille, the 'Don Juan' of Molière, the 'Phèdre' of Racine, and the 'Ruy Blas' of Hugo, while it would also rule out of the English drama the 'Romeo and Juliet,' the 'Hamlet' and the 'Julius Cæsar' of Shakspere. Yet there is significance in the suggestion, nevertheless; and these new Irish plays of Lady Gregory, of Yeats and of Synge, are all the more Irish because they were written by Irishmen on Irish themes and peopled exclusively by Irish characters.

(1914.)

XII

THE CONVENTIONS OF THE MUSIC-DRAMA

I

IN an illuminating criticism of the operas of Puccini, by D. C. Parker, there is a passage which may serve as a text for the present paper. The British writer pointed out that in 'Madame Butterfly' the Italian musician struck out a new line in his choice of a theme, widely different from those which had hitherto appealed to composers, in that he deserted the old world of romanticism and of picturesque villainy, preferring, for the moment at least, a world which is neither old nor romantic and in which the villainy is not picturesque.

"We breathe the air of these times and a modern battleship rides at anchor in the bay. Opera is a convention and a realization of the fact should throw some light on the suitability of subjects. It was not without reason that Wagner insisted upon the value of legendary plots, and I am sure that it is a reliable instinct which whispers to us that there is something wrong when Pinkerton offers Sharpless a whiskey and soda. The golden goblet of the Middle Age, the love-philter of Wagner, we can cheerfully accept. But a decanter and a syphon break the spell and cause a heaviness of heart to true children of the opera-world."

This is sound doctrine, beyond all question; and yet Mr. Parker based it only upon a reliable instinct, without caring to go deeper and to ask why we are willing to quaff a love-philter from the golden goblet and why we hesitate to sip a draught mixt before our eyes from syphon and decanter. Yet he hinted at the reason for our acceptance of the one and for our rejection of the other when he reminded us that "opera is a convention." But it needs more than a realization of this fact to enable us to develop a reliable instinct in regard to the subjects most suitable for operatic treatment. It needs an inquiry into the exact meaning of the word *convention*, as Mr. Parker here employed it. Perhaps we may attain to a solider ground than that supplied by a reliable instinct if we ask ourselves what is the necessity of convention in any of the arts, more particularly in the art of the drama and most particularly in the art of opera.

No doubt, these questions have often been askt and as often answered, altho the responses have not always been wholly satisfactory. This is no bar to a reargument of the case, even if there is no new evidence to be introduced. The French critic was wise as well as witty when he declared that "everything has already been said that could be said; but as nobody listened to it, we shall have to say it all over again." Moreover, very few of us are conscious of the immense number of conventions by means of which we save time and spare ourselves friction in our daily life; and still fewer have taken the trouble to understand either the necessity for these conventions or the basis on which they stand.

A convention is an agreement. In the arts it is an implied contract, a bargain tacit and taken for granted, because it is to the advantage of both parties. In the art of life the spoken word is a convention, and so is the written word. As John C. Van Dyke has aptly put it, in the opening chapter of his suggestive discussion on the 'Meaning of Pictures,' when we wish to convey the idea of water to a friend we do not show him a glass of the fluid, we pronounce the word, which is by agreement the symbol of the thing. If we write it we use five letters, w-a-t-e-r, which bear no likeness whatever to the thing itself, and yet which bring it to mind at once. "This is the linguistic sign for water. The chemical sign for it H_2O, is quite as arbitrary, but to the chemist it means water. And only a little less arbitrary are the artistic signs for it. The old Egyptian conveyed his meaning by waving a zigzag up or down the wall; Turner in England often made a few horizontal scratches do duty for it; and in modern painting we have some blue paint touched with high lights to represent the same thing. None of these signs attempts to produce the original or has any other meaning than to suggest the original. They are signs which have meanings for us only because we agree to understand their meanings beforehand."

If we do not agree to accept the blue paint toucht with high lights or the few horizontal scratches as a proper method of representing water then we deny ourselves the pleasure of marine-painting and of pencil-drawing. The art of the painter is possible only if we are willing to allow him to contradict the facts of nature so that he may delight us with the truth of nature as he sees it. In the preface to his most abidingly popular play, the 'Dame aux Camélias,' the younger Dumas declared that there is "in all the arts a share, larger or smaller but indispensable, which must be left to convention. Sculpture lacks color, painting lacks relief; and they are rarely the one or the other, in the dimensions of the nature they represent. The more richly you bestow on a statue the color of life, the more surely you inflict upon it the appearance of death, because in the rigid attitude to which it is condemned by the material it is made of, it must always lack movement, which even more than color and form is the proof of life."

217

Still more striking is the passage in which the late John La Farge asserted the immitigable necessity of convention in these same twin-arts of painting and sculpture:—"When I work as an artist I begin at once by discarding the way in which things are really done, and translating them at once into another material. Therein consists the pleasure that you and I take in the work of art,—perhaps a new creation between us. The pleasure that such and such a reality gives me and you has been transposed. The great depth and perspective of the world, its motion, its never resting, I have arrested and stopt upon a little piece of flat paper. That very fact implies that I consider the flatness of my paper a fair method of translating the non-existence of *any* flatness in the world that I look at. If I am a sculptor I make for you this soft, waving, fluctuating, colored flesh in an immovable, hard, rigid, fixt, colorless material, and it is this transposition which delights you; (as well as me in a lesser degree who have made it). Therefore at the very outset of my beginning to affect you by what is called the record of a truth, I am obliged to ask you to accept a number of the greatest impossibilities, evident to the senses, and sometimes disturbing, when the convention supposed to be agreed upon between you and myself is understood only by one of the two parties."

II

THESE quotations from La Farge and from Dumas call attention to the essential conditions of the arts of painting and of sculpture,—that the artists do not merely depart from reality, they contradict it absolutely. Only by so contradicting it can they provide us with the specific pleasure that we expect from their respective arts. The portrait painter has to present the head of his sitter motionless on a flat surface and the portrait sculptor has to present the head of his sitter motionless and without color, or rather with the uniform tint of his material, clay or plaster, marble or bronze. And the public accepts these greatest impossibilities not only without protest but without any overt consciousness that they are impossibilities. The public, as a whole, is not aware that it is a party to an implied contract; it is so accustomed to the essential conventions of these two arts that it receives the result of their application as perfectly natural.

In fact, the public can scarcely be said to have made the tacit bargain; rather has it inherited the implied contract from its remotest ancestors, the cave-men who scratched profile outlines on the bones of animals now for centuries extinct. The public is so accustomed to the methods of the painters and of the sculptors that when its attention is called to the fact that it is accepting the greatest impossibilities it is frankly surprized at the unexpected revelation and not altogether pleased. As a whole, the public is not curious to analize the sources of its pleasures; it is perfectly content to enjoy these pleasures without question, as its fathers and its forefathers had enjoyed them century after century. To say this is to say that the fundamental conventions of painting and of sculpture have not been consciously agreed to by the existing public; they have just been taken for granted.

So in like manner have the fundamental conventions of the drama and of the music-drama been taken for granted, generation after generation, altho they involve departures from the fact, contradictions of the fact, impossibilities (to borrow La Farge's exact word) quite as great as those which underly and make possible painting and sculpture. Just as the conventions of the graphic arts were establisht by the cave-dwellers who made the first primitive sketches of the mastodon, so the conventions of the dramatic arts were willingly accepted by the spectators of the earliest dance-pantomime, more or less spontaneously evolved to celebrate the coming of the springtime or the gathering of the harvest.

All the permanent conventions of the drama are accepted by the public because they are for its benefit, to heighten its pleasure, to prevent it from being bored, or even from having its attention distracted by minor things not pertinent to the matter in hand. In real life all stories are straggling; they are involved with extraneous circumstance; and they continue indefinitely into the future as they began indefinitely in the past. The playwright arbitrarily chooses a point of departure; he resolutely eliminates all accompanying circumstances and all environing characters not contributory to the arbitrary end upon which he has decided. He peoples his plot with only the characters absolutely needed; and he conducts his action swiftly from start to finish, heaping situation upon situation, so as to arouse and retain and stimulate the interest of the spectators as the artificially compacted story moves irresistibly and inevitably to its climax.

His characters always make use of his native tongue, which is also the native tongue of the audience. In 'Hamlet' the Danes all speak English; in 'Romeo and Juliet' the Italians all speak English; and in 'Julius Cæsar' the Romans all speak English. Moreover they all make use of an English that no mortal man ever used in real life, not even Shakspere himself. Every one of them always expresses himself accurately and adequately, and completely, with no hesitancies, no repetitions, no fumbling for words; and every one of them apprehends instantly and understands precisely everything that everyone else may say to him. All the language used, whether in prose or in verse, is highly condensed, inexorably compact, transparently clear. There is no need to point out that this is a state of linguistic efficiency unknown in everyday life, filled with the halting babble of a myriad of insignificancies. Yet this departure from reality, this contradiction of the fact, this impossibility, is assented to not only gladly but unthinkingly. The bargain is not consciously made, it is taken for granted, partly because it is for the benefit of the spectators and partly because it is an ancestral inheritance.

These are all essential conventions of the drama, without which it could not exist. They can be found in the plays of every people, ancient or modern, civilized or savage, in the lofty tragedies of Athens, two thousand years ago, as well as in the farces of Paris five hundred years ago. They make possible the drama in prose, the drama in verse, the drama in song, and the drama in gesture. They are the fundamental conventions of the dramatic art, handed down by tradition and certain to survive so long as man shall find delight in the theater, in beholding a story set on the stage to be shown in action before his admiring eyes. From the beginning of things the playwright, like the painter and the sculptor, has always had to ask his audience "to accept a number of the greatest impossibilities."

III

WHILE these are all of them permanent and essential conventions of the drama, there are others peculiar to the music-drama and to it equally necessary, since without them it could not exist,—indeed it could not even have come into being.

We all know that the ordinary speech of man is prose, often careless and inaccurate, ragged and repetitious; and yet if we are to enjoy 'Hamlet' or 'Macbeth' we must accept the impossible supposition that Denmark and Scotland were once inhabited by a race of beings whose customary speech was English blank verse. We all know that the ordinary speech of man is unrhythmic and unrimed; and yet if we are to find pleasure in 'Tartuffe' we must allow that Paris in the reign of Louis XIV was peopled by men and women whose customary speech was the rimed Alexandrine. So the convention which alone makes possible the beautiful art of pantomime—a form of drama restricted in its range but always delightful within its rigid limitations—is that there exists a race of beings who have never known articulate speech, who utter no sounds, and who communicate their feelings and their thoughts by the sole aid of gesture. If we are unwilling to assent to this monstrous proposition we deny ourselves instantly and absolutely all the pleasure that the art of pantomime can bestow.

Now, the convention which supports and makes possible the music-drama is that there is a race of beings whose natural speech is song and only song, with no recourse to merely spoken words. It is by the aid of song alone that the persons who people grand opera can communicate with one another, can transmit information, can express their emotions. Of course, this is a proposition quite as monstrous as that upon which the art of pantomime is based,—or as those upon which the arts of painting and sculpture are founded. It is a proposition which any plain man of everyday common sense is at liberty to reject unhesitatingly; and no one has any right to blame him. All we have a right to do is to point out that the acceptance of this convention is a condition precedent to the enjoyment of opera and that he who absolutely refuses to be a party to the contract thereby deprives himself of all the delights which the music-drama may afford.

Tolstoy was one of those who felt keenly the inherent absurdity of opera, if the test of reality is applied to it,—altho oddly enough he seems never to have become conscious that painting and sculpture are just as remote from the facts of nature. In his curiously individual treatise on 'What is Art?' he narrates his visit to an opera-house while a performance of Wagner's 'Siegfried' was taking place. This music-drama did not interest him, and he held it up to ridicule by the aid of the inexpensive device of satirically narrating the story as it was shown in action, and of describing realistically the appearance and gestures and utterances of the performers. "When I arrived," Tolstoy writes, "an actor sat on the stage amid scenery intended to represent a cave, and before something which was meant to represent a smith's forge. He was drest in tights, with a cloak of skins, wore a wig, and an artificial beard, and with white, weak, genteel hands beat an impossible sword with an unnatural hammer in a way in which no one uses a hammer; and at the same time, opening his mouth in a strange way, he sang something incomprehensible."

This quotation is sufficient to show Tolstoy's unsympathetic attitude and his unwillingness to accept the implied contract which opera calls for. Apparently Tolstoy was present at a performance not as perfect artistically as it ought to have been; but it is equally apparent that he would have been just as hostile if the performance had attained to an ideal perfection. What he was condemning was the music-drama as an art-form; and the animus of his adverse verdict is his unexprest expectation that opera ought to withstand the test of reality. But opera is always unnatural and impossible. It is absurd and monstrous that the dying Tristan's last breath should be powerful enough to reach to the top gallery

225

of a large opera house and that the Rhine-maidens should sing as they are swimming under water; but it is just as unnatural, impossible, absurd and monstrous that Hamlet should speak English blank verse and that the Mona Lisa should be motionless

Here we recall again the final sentence of the pregnant passage earlier quoted from La Farge,—"I am obliged to ask you to accept a number of the greatest impossibilities evident to the senses and sometimes disturbing when the convention supposed to be agreed upon between you and myself is understood only by one of the two parties."

IV

ALTHO the music-drama cannot provide pleasure for those who do not understand the convention or who wilfully refuse to accept it, "the true children of the opera-world," as Mr. Parker felicitously termed them, are so accustomed to this convention that they are rarely conscious of it. Nevertheless they do not wish to be unduly reminded of it and to have their attention called to its various and manifold consequences. Wagner was wise in his generation in preferring to build his plots upon the legends of once-upon-a-time, because it is always easier to make-believe when we allow ourselves to be transported on a magic carpet to that remote, vague

226

and fantastic period. As we know that the Rhine-maidens never existed anywhere or any-when, we never think of cavilling at their ability to sing while they are swimming under water.

But when a battleship swings at anchor and when Pinkerton produces a decanter and syphon to mix a whiskey and soda, we can hardly help being conscious of the artistic impossibility of Pinkerton's extending his invitation in song, which we know not to be the mode of expression natural to an American of our own time asking a friend to take a drink. The sound rule for any artist would seem to be that, whatever his special art, he should carefully avoid everything which tends to awaken in the spectators the consciousness that they are parties to a bargain. The contract holds best when it is implicit, when neither party gives it a thought and when both parties abide by it. "The dramatist," so Lessing declared, "must avoid everything that can remind the audience of their illusion, for as soon as they are reminded, the illusion is gone."

This is the rule that William Gillette broke in his 'Sherlock Holmes', when he allowed one of his characters to describe the invisible fourth wall of the gas-chamber to which the cool and keen-witted detective was to be lured,—that fourth wall which had to be supposed away, so that the audience could hear and see what is taking place upon the stage. This same rule was again violated by Jerome K. Jerome in the 'Passing of the Third Floor Back' and by Barrie in the 'New Word,' when these playwrights set a fender and fire-irons down by the prompter's box, thus asking the spectators to believe that there was an invisible fireplace in the invisible wall.

Nearly a score of years ago I was present at a performance of 'La Traviata' in the opera-house at Vienna; and I was forced to observe the disadvantage of an ill-advised attempt at realistic exactitude in the realm of operatic convention. I had been accustomed to see Verdi's opera set in scenery of no particular place and of no particular period,—and therefore not calling attention to itself; and I was also used to beholding the consumptive heroine arrayed in the very latest Paris gown, while her lovers wore a nondescript costume as dateless and as characterless as the scenery itself. The manager of the Vienna opera-house had unfortunately remembered that Verdi's score was composed to a book made out of the 'Dame aux Camélias' of the younger Dumas, originally performed in Paris in 1852; and therefore he had sought an accurate reproduction of a series of Parisian rooms, with the draperies and the furniture of 1852, while the characters, male and female, lovely heroine and disconsolate lovers, were attired according to the French fashion-plates of that date. In the ballroom scene therefore I beheld all the male members of the chorus habited in the evening dress of 1852 and carrying under their arms the closed crush-hat which had been invented by the ingenious M. Gibus only a little earlier.

And I then had it brought home to me as never before how monstrously impossible the convention of opera is—and must be. I need not say that, as I sat there in the mood of unconscious enjoyment, I regretted having my attention wantonly called to the essential and permanent and inevitable convention by which alone the music-drama is made possible. It struck me not only as unwise but even as a little unfair.

(1917.)

XIII

THE SIMPLIFICATION OF STAGE-SCENERY

I

THIS is a time of unrest in the theater. In almost every modern literature the drama is alive as it was not, half-a-century ago, in any literature except the French. The public is slowly but steadily recovering the lost art of reading plays; and the American public, in particular, is exhibiting a constantly increasing interest in the dramatic literature of other languages, not only French and German, but also Scandinavian and Russian. We are becoming more and more cosmopolitan; and we welcome with equal cordiality the ballet of the Russians and the pantomime of the French. A host of youthful enthusiasts have opened little theaters not only in the leading cities but even in some of the less important towns; and they have made many novel experiments both in the kind of play they have chosen to perform and in the method of presentation. These youthful enthusiasts are abundantly vocal in clamoring for a new departure in dramatic art, boldly demanding the abolition of the hampering traditions of the nineteenth century. Some of them are ready to renounce the heritage of the past, and to venture into the future as upon an uncharted sea. Not a few of them seem to be possest by what the late E. L. Godkin once termed the "common illusion of young men that facility in composition indicates the existence of thought."

Gordon Craig, for example, who is hailed as one of the chief inspirers of the new movement in stage-decoration, is a very radical iconoclast, never concealing his profound dissatisfaction with the achievements of the stage-directors of today. Seemingly he wants the theater to declare its independence of all the other arts, even including literature. At least this appears to be his desire, altho it is not a little difficult to find out from his manifestoes exactly what it is that he wishes. His thoughts, if not hazily held, are obscurely exprest. Seemingly, however, he looks forward to an isolation of the art of the theater as a result of its freeing itself from all entangling alliances and of relying solely on its own resources.

If this really is his aim, its accomplishment would deprive the drama of the aid of literature and reduce it to pantomime,—which was, indeed, its earliest and most primitive form. Now, it ought to be obvious that to force the drama to forego the aid of literature and of all the other arts, is to make it renounce its signal superiority over all these other arts. Music may invite the companionship of lyric poetry and the dance, just as architecture can enrich itself by invoking the assistance of sculpture and of painting. The drama stands alone in its ability to call in the collaboration not of one or two of the sister arts, but of all of them,—music and the song and the dance, painting, sculpture and architecture, even on occasion oratory and the epic. Wagner boldly proclaimed that his music-drama was to be the art-work of the future, simply because it was to be the result of the cordial cooperation of all the nine muses. It is because the drama has never been willing to restrict itself solely to the dramatic that it has achieved its surpassing breadth of appeal.

But if Gordon Craig is not a cogent or a coherent thinker, he is indisputably an artist of undeniable originality, individuality and fertility, as I can testify after a delightful London afternoon spent at an exhibition of his beautiful models. He is dissatisfied with the accepted methods of mounting plays and more especially with the elaborate complexity of the realistic scenery to which the stage-directors of the last two or three generations have accustomed us. He would annihilate both the complexity and the realism, substituting a symbolic simplicity, less expensive and more effective. His designs, if not always practical, have been suggestive; indeed some of those whom he has inspired have been able to achieve results more satisfactory than any he has himself attained. In fact, he is frank in admitting that what he proposes may not be immediately practical, since his designs are only occasionally adjusted to the actual theater of today, some of them being intended for a type of theater which he foresees, and yet others for a theater which he glimpses in his mind's eye and which is never likely to be erected. That is to say, these impractical sets were invented for the sheer delight of the artist himself in their beauty and not for the benefit of future spectators gathered in front of the stage itself.

II

THIS brings us face to face with two questions. First, why are the ardent young enthusiasts so bitterly dissatisfied with the complex and realistic stage-sets to which we are accustomed? And, second, how did the realistic complication of our modern scenery come to be accepted all the world over? The latter had better be answered before the former.

The orchestra of the Greek theater was devoid of scenery and so was the wide and shallow stage of the Roman theater. On the projecting platform of the Tudor theater there were all the properties that might be needful, thrones and

233

beds, well-heads and arbors; but there was no painted scenery. In the theater of Louis XIV there might be scenery of a kind, summary and decorative, rather than characteristic; and the acting took place far in front of the scenery, such as it was, the performer standing well forward between the lines of spectators seated on both sides of the stage and keeping close under the pendent chandeliers that he might be seen. Even on the English stage in the time of Sheridan, the acting was done on the apron curving forward into the audience and lighted by a semi-circle of inadequate oil-lamps. The characters of Sheridan, of Molière and of Shakspere stood nearly all the time; and chairs were provided for them only on the very rare occasions when the plot of the play required them to be seated.

In the eighteenth century the novel had not come into its own; it was held to be so inferior to the drama that it escaped from the control of the codifiers of critical theory. The novelists had often begun as dramatists, Lesage for one and Marivaux for another; and when they wrote fiction they did not feel any more called upon to relate their characters realistically to an appropriate background than they had done when they wrote plays. It is true that Defoe (who had been a journalist), took keen delight in supplying all manner of descriptive details, yet Fielding (who had been a playwright), was not tempted to follow him and was content to project his characters almost in a void, letting them live and move in rooms nearly as bare of furniture and as uncharacteristic as was the stage of the time.

Scott changed all this; he was the earliest of historical novelists; and when he placed his characters in the remote past, he was forced to supply the familiar details of human existence in the period he had chosen for his story. Scott had to do this necessarily, if he wanted to make his readers realize life in some earlier century about which they were likely to know little. Balzac, in his turn, applied the same process to the novel of contemporary life; he described places with intense gusto, revelling in imagining all possible particularities of the town, of the house, and even of the room, in which any one of his more vital characters resided.

The interrelation of prose-fiction and the drama is constant; and just as the novelists of the eighteenth century had been content with the bareness to which they were accustomed in the theater of their own day, so the dramatists of the middle of the nineteenth century began to demand appropriate stage-sets for their intenser social dramas. "An acted play is a novel intensified," said Henry James, "it realizes what the theater suggests, and, by paying a liberal tribute to the senses anticipates your possible complaint

that your entertainment is of the meager sort
styled intellectual." The composers of acted
plays, who knew the abiding effect which Balzac
had achieved by the veracity of his descriptions,
were desirous that the scenery should reinforce
the intellectual appeal of their writing by the sen-
sual of the things seen on the stage.

Fortunately compliance with this demand was
facilitated by a momentous change which took
place in the playhouse in the years when the realistic movement was carrying all before it. In the
course of the middle half of the nineteenth century
the actual stage underwent a transformation.
It was so amply lighted first by gas and then by
electricity, that the actor had no longer to go down
to the footlights to let his changing expression be
seen. The parallel wings and borders by means
of which interiors had been crudely indicated were
abolisht and the compact box-set enabled the
stage-director to suggest more satisfactorily an
actual room. The apron was cut away; and the
curtain rose and fell in a picture-frame. The
characters of the play were thereafter elements in
a picture, which had a characteristic background,
and which might be furnisht with the most realistic elaboration. The former intimacy of the
actor with the spectators, due to his close proximity, disappeared speedily; and with this intimacy
there disappeared also its concomitant, the soliloquy addrest by a character to the audience for

the sole purpose of supplying information. The drama immediately became more pictorial; it could rely more certainly upon gesture; it could renounce the aid of purely rhetorical oratory; it could dispense with description; and it insisted that the performer should subdue himself to those new conditions and to be on his guard lest he should "get out of the picture."

This modification of the physical conditions of performance, which took place between 1850 and 1890, invited the dramatist to deal more directly with life; and it encouraged him to rely more solidly upon the purely dramatic, eschewing the lyric and the epic and seeking solely to present character immesht in situation. It stimulated Ibsen to the acquisition of his masterly technic and it supplied the stage best fitted for his austere inquest upon human nature. Ibsen was as insistent upon the appropriate environment for his characters as was Balzac; and the interior in which he placed any one of his several groups is always vigorously characteristic. The set which he visualized as the fit background for his creatures in the 'Doll's House' would not be appropriate for those in 'Hedda Gabler' or for those in 'Rosmersholm.' Each of these plays has its own dread atmosphere, subtly indicated by significant details.

III

YET Ibsen, even if he was the foremost, was not the only outstanding figure at the beginning of the twentieth century. He was companioned by playwrights as unlike as Rostand and Hauptmann and d'Annunzio. Ibsen, poet as he was beyond all question, wrote prose, compact and direct; he was a realist, altho he was also often a romanticist even in his severer problem-plays. Rostand and Hauptmann and d'Annunzio are rarely realistic; more often than not they are romanticists; and above all they are more frequently poetic. And here we are in sight of an answer to the question early formulated: Why is there so bitter a dissatisfaction with the complex and realistic set to which we have slowly become accustomed? It is because this set, suitable for the staid interiors, wherein the action of the prosaic problem-play is slowly unrolled before it, is less suitable for the out-door scenes of avowedly poetic plays.

The realistic complexity, which elaborates a significant room for the characters of a social drama rooted in fact, cannot attain an equal significance when it seeks to reproduce the haunting landscape of a romantic play flowering out of fantasy. It is appropriate for the 'Ghosts' of Ibsen; but it is not appropriate for the 'Sightless' of Maeterlinck or for the 'As You Like It' of

Shakspere. In a word, the realistic set may be exactly suited to plays of real life, but it does not necessarily suit plays of unreal life illumined by the light that never was on sea or land. Even when 'Twelfth Night' or 'Much Ado About Nothing' is mounted sumptuously and tastefully by a stage-director of the liberality, the ingenuity and the interpreting imagination of Sir Henry Irving, the result is not commensurate with his effort; and the effort itself is often only too visible. The semi-medieval stories which Shakspere adjusted to the jutting platform of the Tudor theater and which are plausible to us now only if we are willing to make believe, have to be taken apart and then put together again in contradiction and almost in defiance of Shakspere's own semi-medieval construction, so that they may be made to adjust themselves to the copiously pictorial method of our modern picture-frame stage. After this inartistic dislocation, they are likely to be overloaded with decorative details not in harmony with their delightful unreality; and the more strenuously the stage-director strives to supply a realistic setting, the less real, the less actual, is the result.

"Of pure poetry there are two kinds," said Lord Dunsany in a preface for a volume of a friend's verses; "that which mirrors the beauty of the world in which our bodies are, and that which builds the more mysterious kingdoms, where geography ends and fairyland begins, with gods and heroes at war, and the sirens singing still, and Alph going down to the darkness from Xanadu." In the modern drama the leader of those whose works mirror the beauty of the world in which our bodies are, is Ibsen; and the foremost representative of those who lay their plays frankly in fairyland is Maeterlinck. It was inevitable that there should be a reaction against the effort to apply the method of complicated realism to plays not compact with reality but compounded of fancy, insubstantial and etherial.

It was inevitable also that a younger generation should welcome a new departure for the presentation of the poetic dramas of Shakspere and would endeavor to discover the means for recapturing something of the simplicity of the original performance, and of avoiding the crushing and needless expense of mechanical realism. Inevitably again the ardor of the youthful leaders of this revolt would tend to be unduly impatient, and to be stimulated by an iconoclastic fervor which might tempt them to a root and branch reform,—to a violent revolution instead of an orderly evolution. They were eager to prove all things and yet they were not always anxious to hold fast that which is true.

What was welcome in the realistic interiors of the problem-plays was the congruity of the background to the temper and tone of the play. The set which Ibsen had visualized for his somber 'Ghosts' was rich in character; it was the fit environment for his disenchanted creatures; it was absolutely congruous with his theme; it served to intensify the appalling action of his tragic story; and it did these things without in any way drawing undue attention to itself. But certain of the sets which Gordon Craig has designed for one or another episode of 'Hamlet' and of 'Macbeth,'—indisputably beautiful in themselves, truly imaginative, superbly decorative,— are not in keeping with the atmosphere of the plays; they are not unobtrusive backgrounds; in fact, they cry aloud to be noticed for their own sake. So it is also with the striking set which he devised for the 'Electra,' bold and massive, but foreign to the spirit of Sophocles, hopelessly un-Greek, and likely to distract the attention of the spectators from the dramatist to the decorator.

As we turn the pages of Gordon Craig's 'Art of the Theater,' delighting in the designs and doing our best to discover his own convictions, we cannot avoid the suspicion that he holds the decorator to be superior to the dramatist and that he believes the control of the theater should pass from the playwright-poet to the painter. Surely it ought to be obvious that the dramatist is the ultimate master of the stage and that the artists whose aid he may invite must be his servants. Beauty of line and of color are in place in the theater only when they contribute to the emotional and intellectual appeal of the play itself; and they are out of place whenever they are permitted to obtrude themselves, to interfere with this appeal and to detract from it.

IV

AFTER the raising of the banner of revolt against the costly and unsatisfactory realistic set, there were many signs of unrest in the theaters of many countries, notably in those of Russia and of Germany. Stage-directors of varying ability ventured upon all sorts of interesting experiments. Some of these novelties approved themselves immediately and won acceptance as tending toward the development of a more satisfactory mode of presenting the poetic drama; but some of them were abhorrent, being incited apparently by an egotistic desire to be different at all costs, to be eccentric or even to be frankly freakish. We find ourselves in a period of transition; and while we are justified in looking forward hopefully, we cannot now clearly descry the goal at the end of the winding path upon which we have entered.

But we know our point of departure, even if we cannot yet foresee where we shall arrive or when; and already can we find full justification for the reaction against the persistent practice of supplying complicated realism for plays the action of which does not take place in the realm of reality. There was, for example, a noble dignity in the bold archway wherewith Sam Hume indicated the city-gate for a Detroit production of Lord Dunsany's 'Tents of the Arabs,' a design which had a distinct beauty of its own but which was also absolutely in keeping with the spirit of the play,—altho a hypercritic might regret that the arch itself was Roman rather than Arabic or even vaguely oriental. Quite as effective in its stark simplicity was the lovely scene designed by Hamilton Bell for the 'Sister Beatrice' of Maeterlinck when it was produced by Winthrop Ames at the New Theater,—a medieval entrance-hall, devoid of all distracting detail and provided with a tall door at the back, ready to open once to reveal the dark sky with its stars shining down on the stalwart figure of the lover come to carry off the enamored nun.

A like feeling for the fitness of things, for the delicately artistic adjustment of the setting to the soul of the play, was discoverable also in the two contrasting scenes which Winthrop Ames caused to be prepared for that enchanting pantomime 'Pierrot the Prodigal.' One of these sets represented the unpretentious home from which the erring son goes forth and to which he returns at last with a broken and a contrite heart,—a low ceilinged room, summarily yet adequately indicated with only the furnishings necessary to the action; and the other set, equally successful in its significance, was the temporary abode of the prodigal when he has yielded to the lure of the lady of pleasure,—a loftier room, seemingly more spacious, sumptuously extravagant in its ornament and yet achieving a character of its own without the aid of a clutter of insignificant details.

The names of the personages and the final flourish of the tricolor flag when the drums rattle past and the fifes shrill out, inform us that the action of 'Pierrot the Prodigal' must be supposed to take place Somewhere In France; and it is also somewhere in France that a certain Man married a Dumb Wife. The vicissitudes of his misadventure were narrated by Rabelais four hundred years ago and they were only recently cast into dialog by Anatole France; yet the infelicitous wedding did not happen in the twentieth century or in the sixteenth, but in the dim and distant epoch known as Once upon a Time. As a matter of fact, the consequences of this marriage are so fantastic, so completely removed from the restraints of reality, that we cannot help knowing that they never did happen anywhere or anywhen,—a knowledge which in no wise interferes with our enjoyment. For this inconsequent impossibility Robert E. Jones

244

invented a sing'e set, at once exterior and interior, charming in color and playful in design, perfectly in accord with the tricksy comicality of the play and reinforcing the humorous unreality of the story. No such house as that which we were invited to gaze upon had ever been built by the hand of man; and yet we accepted it instantly as the only possible habitation for the Man and for his Dumb Wife. In fact, this completely satisfactory setting was designed in perfect accord with the principle this artist has himself declared: "Scenery isn't there to be lookt at, it's really there to be forgotten. The drama is the fire, the scenery is the air that lifts the fire and makes it bright."

The Rabelais-France farce was produced in New York by Granville Barker, and it was by far the most successful of his experiments, several of which were a little too regardless of traditional methods and a little too idiosyncratic in their insistence on novelty for its own sake. The set of the 'Dumb Wife' did not attract attention to itself, whereas in the same manager's production of 'A Midsummer Night's Dream' both the scenes and the costumes shriekt aloud, because they seemed to American audiences out of keeping with the spirit of Shakspere's fairy fantasy. The same criticism would have to be past on the powerfully projected backgrounds which were prepared by Golsovine for a Russian production of the 'Festin de Pierre' and which were not consonant with the restrained tone of Molière's version of the Don Juan story, altho they might have been in place if used to adorn the lyric melodrama of Tirso de Molina, the remote original of Molière's piece.

v

IN the immediate future it is probable that the poetic drama, Shakspere's or Maeterlinck's, will be presented in our theaters far less realistically and far less expensively. We shall no longer expect a spectacle as glittering, as costly and as cumbrous as the reproduction of Paul Veronese's 'Marriage at Cana' which Augustin Daly bestowed upon the final act of the 'Taming of the Shrew.' It is also probable that this simplification, this renunciation of ultra-realism, this substitution of indication, summary but adequate, for actual representation, may in time affect even the mounting of modern plays in prose. This will not necessarily prove to be an improvement. A British critic once found fault with Ibsen because he used the fittest words and not the most beautiful; and Ibsen insisted on the fittest backgrounds for his social dramas, and not the most beautiful. In the mounting of the modern problem-play what is essential is not beauty for its own sake, but character.

246

There is always danger that the effort to
achieve the characteristic may over-reach itself
with disastrous results. In a letter to Sarcey on
the art of stage-management Dumas fils recorded
his preference for a very simple interior with as
little furniture as possible, all in neutral tones,
against which the personages would stand out in
vigorous relief; and he was not at all pleased
with the single set which Montigny devised for
the three acts of 'Monsieur Alphonse.' As the
action took place in the country-house of a
retired naval officer, the manager imagined a
room with an exotic decoration vaguely Chinese
and with bamboo furniture, most of which was
painted a brilliant red. "The effect was original
and gay, when the stage was empty; but none
the less it suggested a bird-cage . . . and one
was moved to wonder whether the persons of the
play would not sooner or later begin to hop from
perch to perch."

Dumas, a born playwright, demanded always
that the decorative should be subordinate to the
dramatic. "If we insist on being original, and
on being different, we are in imminent danger of
being eccentric and of bringing about an antagonism between the subject of the play and its
scenery." It was this unfortunate desire to be
original and to be different which recently misled an American manager into entrusting a New
York house-decorator with the designing of the

successive sets for the 'New York Idea.' Langdon Mitchell's heroine in the first act is about to marry into a family of hereditary dulness; and being herself a delightfully lively person, she returns, in the last act, to the husband she has divorced. But the uninspired house-decorator did not provide the opening act with an interior of transcendent respectability nor did he bestow upon the closing scene an interior of contrasting levity. There was not actual antagonism between the subject of the play and its scenery, but there was certainly no harmony. The interiors were in no wise characteristic of the persons who were supposed to live in them; in fact the only character that they had was that of the house-decorator's own shop.

No such blunder was made by David Belasco in the single set of the 'Return of Peter Grimm'—perhaps the most extreme example of realistic complexity, with its unending details, all characteristic, all unobtrusive and all congruous with the topic of the play. The room which the author-manager set before us is the room in which Peter Grimm would live; it is the house in which he would die; and it is the home to which he would return after death. The atmosphere of the whole dwelling, as we breathe it, is in perfect accord with the appealing personality of the forlorn ghost. To simplify this set would be to deprive it of the value given to it by the intuition and the dexterity of its designer.

Yet Belasco, always alert to perceive the possibilities of every new development in the art of the stage, has more recently bestowed upon 'Marie-Odile' a very simple setting in accord with its simpler theme; and so dexterously did he select the sparse elements of this rarer and less encumbered scene, that there was no diminution in the pictorial support of the story. In both cases Belasco workt in obedience to the unchanging law which declares that it is the perfection of a woman's dress to make its wearer look her best without in any way attracting attention to itself.

The dominating principle in putting a drama on the stage is plain enough. Every play ought to be provided with the specific background which will best serve to bring out its own special quality. A brilliant comedy of modern society like Clyde Fitch's 'Truth' will call for a scenic investiture more complex than would be appropriate for a fleeting episode like Lady Gregory's 'Rising of the Moon.'

It is not often that the author himself is as willing to leave the choice of method to the producer as Echegaray disclosed himself to be in the directions prefixt to his one-act piece, the 'Street Singer':—"The stage represents a square or a street. There may or may not be trees;

there may or may not be seats; there may or may not be lighted lamps. The only thing which is essential is the wall of a house facing the spectators so that the Beggars and the Singer may take their places against it. The time is night."

(1918.)

XIV

THE VOCABULARY OF THE SHOW–BUSINESS

I

EVERY art has, and has to have, its own special and highly specialized vocabulary, ample for its own needs and therefore abounding in words and terms and phrases, often startlingly strange to those who are unfamiliar with the technicalities devised by its practitioners. The electricians, for example, make use of a heterogeny of vocables unknown to the profane and sometimes fearfully and wonderfully made. I recall that I once saw in an electrical weekly an advertisement asserting the superiority of the manufacturer's "separately excited *boosters*"; and when I consulted an electrical expert he informed me that these were very useful machines and that their name exactly described their purpose. This explanation did not lift me out of my ignorance; but when it was too late to retaliate I wondered whether I could not have had him at an equal disadvantage if I had askt him if he knew what a *star-trap* was or a *raking-piece,* a *run-down* or a *baby-spot.* I think that he would have been as

251

much puzzled by these terms, well-known to all who are wont to pass thru the stage-door, as I was bewildered by the excitability of boosters.

The theater has an elaborate terminology of its own, completely adequate to its manifold necessities, and as precise in its meaning and as accurate in its application as the vocabulary of any of the sciences. To the outsider the technicalities of the stage are likely to be as mysterious as those of any other department of human activity,—as mysterious and as misleading. A *star-trap*, for example, is not intended for the sole use of a star ; on the contrary it is a mechanical device the obvious dangers of which no star would ever be called upon to risk. A *baby-spot* carries with it no suggestion that a stage infant is about to break out with the measles; and a *run-down* does not imply that anybody is in need of medical treatment. Nor has a *raking-piece* anything whatever to do with gardening.

In the prosaic eighteenth century, it was held to be good form in speaking and in writing to use general terms so far as possible and to avoid the use of specific technicalities. But in our more imaginative twentieth century we relish the exact word and we delight in employing it with absolute scientific precision. Rudyard Kipling revealed himself as a man of his own time when he made use of the special terms of engineering, as he did in prose in '007' and in verse in 'M'An-

drews' Hymn.' Perhaps no other of our poets
and story-tellers has gone so far in this direction
as Kipling; and yet many of them are tending
that way, to the constant enrichment of our everyday speech as this is necessarily replenisht from
the highly specialized vocabularies of the several
arts and sciences.

It is not uncommon to hear the technicalities
of the theater contemptuously thrust aside as
merely the slang of the stage. Now, no doubt,
the stage has its slang; indeed, there is no denying that stage-folk are plentifully supplied with
the fleeting phrases which may fairly be dismist as slang. But none the less has the theater
a vocabulary of its own, as rigid in its meaning
and as legitimate in its usage as the vocabulary
of electricity or of architecture. No one is justified in denouncing *baby-spot* and *star-trap*,
raking-piece and *run-down* as specimens of
merely ephemeral slang. These terms have a
scientific precision as indisputable as *horse-power*
or *foot-ton* or *kilo-watt;* they are as necessary
and they are as deserving of collection and of
definition as the terms of painting or of sculpture,
of chemistry or of medicine.

It is a curious thing that these technicalities
of the theater are only a few of them to be found
even in the largest and most comprehensive of
the dictionaries of the English language; and it
is even more curious that they have never been

assiduously selected and set in order in a subordinate dictionary of their own. Similar vocabularies have been prepared for the art of painting, for example, and for the science of medicine; and an ample proportion of the specific terms of painting and of medicine have been included in the larger dictionaries of the language as a whole. It is to be hoped that some man of letters, some journalist intimately acquainted with the things of the theater, may some day be moved to undertake the task of preparing a stage-glossary, of collecting and of defining the vocabulary of the arts of the stage—playwriting, acting, scene-painting, stage-management.

II

THE task will prove to be more arduous and more onerous than would appear at first sight, since it ought not to be limited to the theater itself but should be made to include also the special vocabularies of all the other departments of the show-business, not only pantomime and dancing, but the circus and negro-minstrelsy, the variety-show and the moving-picture. Each of these departments of the show-business has words and phrases of its own, many of them more or less unknown in the others and all of them needing explanatory definition. We want to be able to turn to this glossary for the precise description of *Leotard-body*, for example, and of *Risley-act*.

We shall be glad to have an exact explanation of the circus-act known as "Pete Jenkins,"—most humorously described by Mark Twain in 'Huckleberry Finn.' And how many of us know what a *tranka* is or how the *batoute* of the circus differs from the springboard of the gymnasium? We may be able to guess at the meaning of *big top,* and of *canvas-man;* we may hazard a conjecture as to the exact significance of *giant-swing* and of *muscle-grind;* but not a few of us would grope in the dark vainly if we were suddenly asked for an explanation of *lashells* (which are the ropes making taut the rod wherefrom a trapeze is suspended). Then there is *mechanic,* which the outsider recognizes as a name applied to a human being and which the circus insider knows as the name of a machine used in the training of riders for the ring.

However outlandish these terms may seem to those inexperienced in the life led by the itinerant tent-dwellers, they are so familiar and so usual to the circus man that he would probably be surprised to learn that they were unfamiliar to the immense majority of mankind who are only spectators of the sports of the arena and not participants therein. Altho the circus has a host of these special terms, perhaps more than any other subdivision of the show-business except the theater itself, other subdivisions have also their full share. While the vogue of the circus reveals no sign of diminishing, the popularity of negro-minstrelsy has undergone an eclipse in recent years. Half-a-century ago there were two dozen or two score troupes touring the country season after season, whereas there are now fewer than half-a-score and perhaps even fewer than a scant half-dozen.

No longer does the big drum invite us to "40. Count them. 40" and very rarely do we listen to the preliminary request of the *middleman:* "Gentlemen, be seated!" Only occasionally now do we see the the semi-circle of burnt-cork countenances with the unfailingly dignified *interlocutor* in the center and with Bones and Tambo at the extremities. Here in the United States, where negro-minstrelsy was born, Bones and Tambo are known as *end-men,* whereas in Great Britain, to which the black-face entertainment was transported early in its career, they are always called *corner-men.* Not often now does the First Part end with the accustomed *walk around;* and only infrequently in these days is the Second Part described as an *olio.* Still rarer is our opportunity to behold the *break-down,* rendered more difficult and more amazing by the use of *flappers,* or to gaze delighted on a *statue clog-dance,* with its rhythm tinklingly accentuated by the employment of *clinkers.* Vanisht also is the street parade which made it necessary that the players of the stringed instruments should be able to *double in brass*, as the advertisements insisted.

III

THE picturesqueness of the vocabulary of the circus and of the minstrel-show is undeniable; and those of us who are keenly interested in the multiform developments of the English language cannot fail to regret that this vocabulary has not received from the lexicographers the attention it deserves. Probably the most obvious reason for their neglect is their ignorance of its existence. The most obvious of reasons for their ignorance is that the technical terms of the several subdivisions of the show-business do not often find themselves set down in black and white. They exist and they survive by word of mouth only; and there is rarely any actual need to write them down. Even when they may get themselves written out, this is likely to be only in a temporary list drawn up by a prompter or a stage-manager. Of course, they are freely employed in the friendly letters of the stage-folk one to another. But these letters and these lists, when they have served their immediate purpose, are very unlikely to get into print or even to be preserved.

Not often actually written, the technicalities of the theater even less frequently appear on the printed page where they might chance to meet the eye of the dictionary-maker. Doubtless, there are a host of stage-terms which have been used orally for years without ever finding themselves in print. Thus it is that they have never had a chance to excite the curiosity of the lexicographers. The vocabularies of engineering and of medicine are preserved in the many text-books constantly pouring from the press for the benefit of the students of these two arts; and so it is that they are brought to the attention of the alert scouts of linguistic research, always desirous of multiplying the number of new words to be included in the newest editions and in the latest supplements of their dictionaries. But no college has yet been tempted to give a course in stage-craft; and there are no technical schools requiring text-books for the instruction of novices in the various branches of the show-business. There are examinations for the license to practise law and medicine; but admission to all the departments of the show-business is free. The stage-door stands open to all, no diploma being demanded from actor or acrobat, dancer or pantomimist.

It is true that the vocabulary of the show-business is necessarily employed more or less by writers of fiction when they venture to take their heroes and their heroines from among the show-folk. But the novelists who have chosen to deal with life behind the scenes are rarely equipt with an intimate knowledge of that dim region and

258

they are not likely to feel themselves called upon
to present the everyday details of the theatrical
career with the aid of the special vocabulary of
the stage. I suppose that I must have read at
least a hundred stories of theatrical life, long and
short; and I doubt if there could be gleaned from
them all more than half-a-hundred of the technical terms of the theater. And while novels of
the stage are many, novels of the circus are few
and novels of the minstrel-show are non-existent.
Just at present the writers of fiction seem to have
a particular fancy for the moving-picture; and
they are making plain to new readers the methods
and the mysteries of the art of the screen, still
in process of rapid development. These readers
are enlightened as to the heroine's endeavor to
register her swiftly changing emotions and as
to her efforts to avoid *wasting film*. They are
told what a *close-up* is; they are informed as to
the precise moment when the director tells the
camera-man to *shoot*; and they may even be
instructed as to the meaning of a necessary but
entirely new verb made out of an old noun,—the
verb *to panoram*.

IV

RAPIDLY expanding as the vocabulary of the
moving-picture studio may be, rich as the vocabulary of the variety-show may be, ample
as the vocabulary of the circus already is,

no one of them is as full and as varied as the vocabulary of the theater itself,—a vocabulary having its remoter origins in the rude mysteries of the Middle Ages, expanding steadily in the professional playhouse of Elizabeth and James, enlarging itself again in the roofed and artificially lighted theaters of the Restoration, gaining a further elaboration in the eighteenth-century theater with the development of scene-painting by De Loutherburg, and attaining to its present complexity after the invention of the electric light had aided in the substitution of our present picture-frame stage for the apron-stage of a hundred years ago.

The unlearned reader of Henslowe's diary is likely to wonder what matter of property it was which he there finds catalogued as "*1 Hell-mouth.*" The inquiring reader of Ford's plays is interested to discover that this dramatist in one of his pieces calls for the use of a "chair with an *engine,*"—the context making it evident that this was a trick-chair, with concealed arms which flew forward to imprison the unsuspicious sitter whenever the villain released the secret spring. The intelligent reader of Shakspere who abandons our misleading library editions, with their modernized stage-directions, and who turns to the original folios and quartos, can gather a significant collection of Elizabethan stage-technicalities, which he will find helpful to a proper understanding of the conditions of theatrical performance in Tudor days. In 'Julius Cæsar,' for example, when the time comes for Mark Antony to deliver his address to the Roman populace we are informed that "he goes up into the *pulpit*"—that is to say into a crude and conventionalized rostrum perfectly satisfactory to the groundlings who stood restless in the unroofed yard.

This intelligent reader of Shakspere may however find himself a little at a loss when he comes to the 'Taming of the Shrew' and when he finds that at a certain moment the stage-direction declares "enter the drunkard *above*." The context however will make it plain that the drunkard is Christopher Sly; and any text-book of the Tudor theater will inform him that "to enter above" meant to appear in the gallery over the stage so that the actor could look down on the action taking place on the broad platform below. The Elizabethan "to enter above" must not be confounded with our modern "to go up stage" which means to go further back from the footlights just as "to come down" means to approach them. If however this Shaksperian reader meets with the unfamiliar word *traverse*, he will consult the text-books in vain for a satisfactory explanation, since we have not yet ascertained exactly what kind of a scenic appliance this term designated.

The compiler of the much to be wisht for historical dictionary of theatrical terms, ancient and modern, will make it plain that the word *clown* did not connote to the Elizabethans what it did to the Victorians. It did not mean an acrobatic humorist of the circus or a comic character in a pantomime. It was in fact almost the exact equivalent of *low comedian*, of the performer who undertakes the broadly comic parts, the accepted funmaker of the company, certain to provoke a ready laugh merely by his welcome appearance even before he has crackt his first joke. That there were recognized "lines of business" in the English theater while Shakspere was writing for it is indisputable; but except in this single case of the *clown* we do not know what they were called. It seems likely that in the company of the Globe theater Condell played *heavies* and that some unidentified but brilliant performer was entrusted with the *light-comedy* parts. But we have no information as to the names given to these two lines of business or even if they had then any specific name. As the Tudor actors had become professional only a few years before Shakspere went on the stage, it is probable that they had not yet been forced to invent a long list of technical terms, altho they must have had many which have not come down to us.

V

In the course of the past three centuries and
a half the theater has solidly establisht itself;
it has undergone many changes; and its vocabulary has been multiplied in response to varying conditions. Shakspere was used to an octag-
onal playhouse, open to the sky, with a platform
jutting into the yard. His stage was encumbered
by the gallants who sat on both sides, smoking
their long pipes. It had abundant properties but
it had absolutely no scenery, as we now understand the word. The machinery was extremely
simple and primitive. As the playwrights sought
for as much spectacle as was possible on their
bare stage, and as they delighted in storms—
there are three of these in 'King Lear,'—probably
their theater had devices akin to the *wind-
machine* and the *thunder-barrel*. But Shakspere
would be badly puzzled if he could come back to
hear a producer of our own time talk about the
wings or the *flies*, about *tormentors* and *border-
lights*, about *panorama-grooves* and *cyclorama-
drops*.

While Shakspere could not possibly have foreseen these terms descriptive of our latter-day
complexity of stage-decoration, he would find
it easy enough to arrive at the significance of
phrases which dealt rather with the art of the
actor. He would not take long to ascertain that

263

one performer confines himself to *straight business* or that another performer had a part that *played itself*. He would appreciate the compliment when he was assured that certain plays of his, 'Hamlet' for one and 'As You Like It' for another, were *actor-proof*. He would be inclined to praise the actor, who was always *letter-perfect*, who never failed to *get a hand*, whose popularity was so great that no piece in which he appeared was ever a *frost*, and whose memory was so good that he never *dried up*.

Men who rarely or never enter the theater will be found declaring that a certain politician is only an *understudy*, altho he is always seeking to get himself in the *spotlight*, thereby making a *three-ring circus* of himself. In an incriminating letter one American statesman asserted that he would not be found "a *dead head* in the enterprize"; and another American statesman, when he was a candidate for the presidency, was loudly advertized as "the *advance-agent* of prosperity."

(1917.)

XV

MATTHEW ARNOLD AND THE THEATER

I

THOSE of us who are now sexagenarians and who had the good fortune to make acquaintance with 'Essays in Criticism' in our undergraduate days and to read the successive collections of Matthew Arnold's later criticisms as they appeared one by one in the score of years that followed, can never forget the debt we owe to the critic who opened our eyes to the value of culture, to the purpose of criticism and to the duty of "seeing the thing as it is." We felt an increasing stimulus as we came to know Arnold's writings more intimately, as we absorbed them, as we made his ideas our own, as we sought to apply his principles and to borrow his methods. The influence of Arnold's work upon the generation born in the middle of the nineteenth century was immediate and it has been enduring.

"Without in the least over-rating himself," so Brownell has finely phrased it, Arnold "took himself with absolute seriousness, and his work from first to last is informed with the high sincerity of a consistent purpose—the purpose of being nobly useful to his time and country by preaching to men precisely the gospel he conceived they most vitally needed. For the consideration of his public and his era he deemed energy less important than light, earnestness less needful than sweetness, genius less beneficent than reasonableness, erudition less called for than culture." He preacht always persuasively, making his points sharply and often tipping them with wit that they might penetrate the more swiftly. He knew so certainly what he wanted to prove that it was easy for him always to be clear. His style, one of the most delightful in the whole range of English literature, is ever limpid, pellucid, transparent.

As he was directly addressing the public of his own era, he constantly dealt with the themes of immediate interest to his contemporaries in his own country. So it is that a large proportion of his writing, always indisputably literary in its treatment, is now discovered to be sometimes journalistic in its theme. Whatever interest his discussion of the Burials Bill, and of the Deceased Wife's Sister's Bill, may have had when these topics were being hotly debated in the House of Commons, has evaporated now that the passage of years has deprived them of their pertinency. Moreover, even in writing his essays on questions of permanent importance, the question of secondary education, for example, and the question of the classics against the sciences,

Arnold was so eager to catch the attention of his contemporaries that he never hesitated to make use of illustrations from the happenings of the moment, likely to be a little unintelligible to readers of a later generation.

To say this is to suggest that he yielded a little too much and a little too often to the temptation of an instantaneous and fleeting effect, and that there are passages in his writings, and not a few of them, which will be obscure to readers of the twentieth century without an annotation almost as abundant as that which does not prevent Pope's 'Dunciad' from being unreadable. The fact is that Arnold, although essentially a man of letters, had a hankering after the newspaper, after the direct and evanescent impression of journalism. His essays were publisht in magazines and reviews; and the magazine,—and the review also—is always alert to capture the element of timeliness; it is at best only a bridge between literature and journalism. 'Friendship's Garland,' one of the most amusing of Arnold's books and one in which he most completely exprest certain of his opinions, was originally contributed to a daily paper, the *Pall Mall Gazette*, at irregular intervals during the years 1866 to 1870. It is true that the *Pall Mall Gazette*, while under the control of its founder, Frederick Greenwood, and afterward when it was edited by John Morley, was the most literary of London

267

journals, rivalling in this respect the *Temps* and the *Débats* of Paris. To this evening journal, appealing to the better sort of newspaper readers, Arnold continued to contribute from time to time brief articles on literary and educational topics, most of which he did not care to preserve in his successive volumes, and only half-a-dozen of which have been included even in the more or less complete *édition de luxe* of his prose and verse publisht in fifteen volumes in 1903–4 and limited to seven hundred and fifty copies.

Among these newspaper contributions rescued in this limited edition are a valuable note on George Sand (whom he rated higher than Balzac), and a series of five letters from 'An Old Playgoer,' written between December, 1882, and October, 1884. These five letters represent his sole venture into the field of theatrical criticism, —excepting only the very interesting paper on the 'French Play in London,' evoked by the visit of the Comédie-Française to England in 1879. This single essay and these five brief letters are the only evidences of Arnold's keen interest in the theater. He was a constant playgoer,—unlike Sainte-Beuve, in whose footsteps he followed loyally and who seems to have cared little for the acted drama, altho he was always characteristically acute and felicitous in his criticism of Molière and of the other masters of the French stage.

Born in 1822, Matthew Arnold was old enough to have witnessed the final appearances of the last of the Kemble brotherhood; and in one of the *Pall Mall Gazette* letters he recorded his opinion that the Benedick of Charles Kemble was superior to that of Henry Irving. "I remember how in my youth," he confest in his paper on the performances of the Comédie-Française, "after a first sight of the divine Rachel at the Edinburgh theater, in the part of Hermione, I followed her to Paris, and for two months never missed one of her performances." No doubt it was this intensive study of the great actress which inspired his three noble sonnets on Rachel.

One can glean from his publisht correspondence a sparse record of his occasional visits to the theater in England and on the continent,— records often accompanied by his off-hand judgments of the plays and of the players whom he beheld. In February, 1861, he saw Charles Fechter as Othello: "the first two acts I thought poor (Shakspere's fault, partly), the next two effective, and the last pretty well." In April, 1864, he accepted an invitation to see Kate Bateman as Leah, adding that he had already seen "most of the things that are being given now." In March, 1865, he went with his family to see Sothern as Lord Dundreary. In November, 1874, he writes that he much wanted to see 'Hamlet' (which Irving was then acting); and in

February, 1876, he tells his sister that he is going
to see "that gibbering performance, as I fear it is,
Irving's Othello." Nearly ten years later in
November, 1885, he saw 'Othello' at the Royal
Theater in Berlin: —"horrid! but I wanted for
once to see Shakspere in German." And a year
after, in March, 1886, when he was again in Germany, he reported that he was going "a great deal
to the theaters, the acting is so good" (this was
in Munich).

II

IN 1856, when he was thirty-four, he seems to
have planned a closet-drama on a Roman theme;
"I am full of a tragedy of the time of the end of
the Republic—one of the most colossal times of
the world, I think. . . . It won't see the light,
however, before 1857." It never has seen the
light; and when 1857 arrived it found him at
work on a closet-drama on a Greek theme, the
'Merope' which he was to publish in 1858. As he
was engaged in rehandling a story already dealt
with by Euripides, Maffei, Voltaire and Alfieri,
Arnold wisely undertook an analysis of the
dramaturgic methods of the greatest and the most
skilful of all the Attic dramatists: "what I learn
in studying Sophocles for my present purpose is,
or seems to me, wonderful; so far exceeding all
that one would learn in years' reading of him without such a purpose."

270

In the preface to his collected 'Poems,' issued in 1853, he had discust the poet's choice of a theme. He did not cite but he echoed Voltaire's assertion that the success of a tragedy depends on its subject. In fact, Arnold is discussing poetry at large and not dramatic poetry only, yet the principle he laid down applies with special force to the drama: "the poet has in the first place to select an excellent action; and what actions are the most excellent? Those, certainly, which most powerfully appeal to the great primary human affections: to those elementary feelings which subsist permanently in the race, and which are independent of time."

In the preface to 'Merope' itself, written five years later, Arnold sought to justify his selection of a Greek action, and his attempt to present this action as he imagined it would have been presented by a Greek dramatist. He described the origin and development of Greek tragedy, proving his knowledge of its principles. Yet in the play itself he was unable to apply these principles successfully. He lackt both the native dramatic genius and the acquired theatrical talent. In a letter of February, 1858, to his sister, he exprest his dissatisfaction with the adverse criticisms of his dramatic poem, which were the result largely of his own argumentative preface: "Instead of reading it for what it is worth, everybody begins to consider whether it does not betray a design to substitute tragedies *à la grecque* for every other kind of poetical composition in England, and falls into an attitude of violent resistance to such an imaginary design. What I meant them to see in it was a specimen of the world created by the Greek imagination. This imagination was different from our own, and it is hard for us to appreciate, even to understand it; but it had a peculiar power, grandeur, and dignity, and these are worth trying to get an apprehension of."

What Arnold himself failed to perceive is that the peculiar power, grandeur and dignity of the Greek imagination can best be apprehended by a study of the tragedies written by the Greeks themselves and that there was no need for him or for any other Englishman to try to beat the Attic tragedians on their own ground and with their own weapons. After all, the most satisfactory Greek tragedies are and must be those written by the Greeks, as the most satisfactory Elizabethan dramas are those written by the Elizabethans. The action of 'Merope' might be excellent; it might "most powerfully appeal to the great primary human affections"; but it could exert this appeal upon a modern audience only if it were presented in accord with modern conditions. The theme of 'Merope' might have a universal and perennial interest, but the form which Matthew Arnold gave it was only local and temporary, however superb it might have been when it had evolved spontaneously from the special conditions of theatrical performance in Athens. Furthermore, with all his liking for the acted drama, Arnold in composing 'Merope' was not thinking of performance in any theater, he was creating only a closet-drama, a still-born offspring of the Muse. A play which is not intended to be played is a contradiction in terms; it is an overt absurdity, no matter how greatly gifted the poet may be who deceives himself in the vain effort to achieve the truly dramatic without taking into account the theater, in which only can the true drama be born.

Eight years later he seems to have been on the verge of repeating his blunder and of again wasting his effort in an attempt foredoomed to failure. In March, 1866, he wrote to his mother that he was troubled to find that Tennyson was at work on a subject, the story of the Latin poet Lucretius, which he himself had been occupied with for some twenty years: "I was going to make a tragedy out of it. . . . I shall probably go on with it, but it is annoying, the more so as I cannot possibly go on at present so as to be ready this year, but must wait till next." Fortunately for himself he did not go on; and before the next year came the project of a tragedy on Lucretius had joined the earlier project of the tragedy "of the time of the end of the Republic." In the first planned dramatic poem there might have been the

273

stuff out of which a true tragedy could be made,
even if Arnold was not the man to make it; but
the subject of the later Roman poem seems hopelessly infertile. It is true that Molière was intensely interested in Lucretius, and Molière was a
born playwright; but all that Molière planned to
do was to make a French translation of the great
work of Lucretius; and the Latin poet would
never have suggested himself to the French dramatist as the possible hero of a tragedy.

III

WITH Arnold's persistent desire to use the dramatic form, with his lively curiosity as to the principles of playmaking and with his unfailing interest in the art of acting, we may well wonder
why it is that no one of his more elaborate critical
studies was devoted to any of the great dramatists.
There are the lofty sonnets on Sophocles and on
Shakspere; but there is no single study of Sophocles or of Shakspere or of Molière. Scattered
thru his essays are many penetrating bits of
criticism upon one or another of the playwrights
of Europe. In the essay, 'A French Critic on
Goethe,' for example, there is an illuminating
comparison of Goethe's 'Goetz von Berlichingen'
with Schiller's 'Robbers.' Arnold quoted the
assertion of a British critic that "there was something which prevented Goethe from ever becom-

ing a great dramatist; he could never lose himself sufficiently in his creations." And on this
Arnold commented that it is in 'Goetz' that
Goethe loses himself most. 'Goetz' is full of
faults, " but there is a life and a power in it,
and it is not dull. This is what distinguishes
it from Schiller's 'Robbers.' The 'Robbers' is at
once violent and tiresome. 'Goetz' is violent,
but it is not tiresome."

The one long article devoted exclusively to
things theatrical is the 'French Play in London,'
written in 1879, and reprinted in 'Irish Essays,'—
a volume in which it finds itself strangely out of
place in its enforced companionship with half-a-
dozen sprightly specimens of political polemic.
The 'French Play in London' is one of the cleverest of Arnold's essays, and one of the most charming. It is also one of the most valuable, rich
in matter, graceful and urbane in manner, witty
in expression and wise in outlook. It reveals
Arnold's genuine appreciation of the drama as a
literary form,—and it discloses also his understanding of the art of acting, by which only is the
drama made vital.

The Comédie-Française was then in the pleni-
tude of its superiority over all other histrionic ag-
gregations. It possest a company of comedians
probably unequalled in France before or since, and
certainly unequalled in England,—except possibly
at Drury Lane in the early years of Sheridan's

management, when the 'School for Scandal' was "in all its glory," as Charles Lamb said. The boards of the Théâtre Français were nightly trod by Got and Coquelin, by Thiron, Barré and Febvre, by Sarah-Bernhardt and Croizette, by Barretta and Jouassain. In comedy, in Molière, Beaumarchais and Augier, it was incomparable; in Hugo it was superb; and even if it was not so superb in Corneille and Racine, it was at least far more than adequate.

Although Arnold began by declaring that he did not propose to analize the artistic accomplishment of the several members of this galaxy of stars, he did allow himself one excursus into purely histrionic criticism,—an excursus which proved both his insight and his foresight. He pointed out—and this was in 1879—the fatal defect in the equipment of Sarah-Bernhardt, a defect which was to be made painfully manifest in the ensuing thirty years:—"One remark I will make, a remark suggested by the inevitable comparison of Mlle. Sarah-Bernhardt with Rachel. One talks vaguely of genius, but I had never till now comprehended how much of Rachel's superiority was purely in intellectual power, how eminently this power counts in the actor's art as in all arts, how just is the instinct which led the Greeks to mark with a high and severe stamp the Muses. Temperament and quick intelligence, passion, nervous mobility, grace, smile, voice, charm, poetry,—Mlle. Sarah-Bernhardt has them all. One

watches her with pleasure, with admiration,—
and yet not without a secret disquietude. Something is wanting, or, at least, not present in
sufficient force, something which alone can secure
and fix her administration of all the charming
gifts which she has, can alone keep them fresh,
keep them sincere, save them from perils by ca-
price, perils by mannerism. That something is
high intellectual power. It was here that Rachel
was so great; she began, one says to oneself as
one recalls her image and dwells upon it,—she
began almost where Mlle. Sarah-Bernhardt ends."

A little later in his essay, Arnold, as was his
wont, and in accord with what Brownell has called
his "missionary spirit," askt what was the moral
to be drawn by us who speak English from the
opportunity to study the best that the French
stage had to offer. He digrest to point out that
Victor Hugo is not "a poet of the race and lineage
of Shakspere", as Swinburne had rashly asserted
in one of his characteristically dithyrambic rhap-
sodies. Arnold dwelt also on the inferiority of the
rimed French alexandrine to English blank verse
and to the Greek iambic as a poetic instrument
for dramatic use. "Victor Hugo is said to be
a cunning and mighty artist in alexandrines,
and so unquestionably he is; but he is an artist
in a form radically inadequate and inferior, and
in which a drama like that of Sophocles or
Shakspere is impossible."

Then Arnold, writing in 1879, it must be again

recalled, declared that "we in England have no modern drama at all. We have our Elizabethan drama" and eighteenth-century comedy. "Then we have numberless imitations and adaptations from the French. All of these are at bottom fantastic,"—because the result of putting French wine into English bottles is to give to the attentive observer "a sense of incurable falsity in the piece as adapted." To this point Arnold was to recur again in one of his 'Letters of an Old Playgoer.' Yet even at this moment, when the English language had no drama dealing with life of the English-speaking peoples, these peoples were revealing a steadily increasing interest in the theater. " I see our community turning to the theater with eagerness, and finding the English theater without organization or purpose, or dignity,—and no modern English drama at all except a fantastical one. And then I see the French company from the chief theater of Paris showing themselves to us in London,—a society of actors, admirable in organization, purpose and dignity, with a modern drama not fantastic at all, but corresponding with fidelity to a very palpable and powerful ideal."

He askt "What is the consequence which it is right and rational for us to draw? Surely it is this: 'The theater is irresistible; *organize the theater.*'" And then he outlined a method of organization which would provide London with a company of actors worthy of consideration by the side of the company which had come over from Paris. When this is once done a modern drama "will also, probably, spring up";—that is to say, Arnold hoped that an adequate and working organization of the theater would bring about a new birth in the English drama. And the event proved that the second of these hopes was to be fulfilled without being preceded by any effort to attain the first. The English theater is not yet "organized" in accord with Arnold's suggestions; but the English language has develupt a modern drama, not adapted from the French and therefore not fantastic at all, but corresponding with more or less fidelity to a palpable and powerful ideal. The beginnings of this revivification of the English drama were already visible in 1879, altho they were a little more obviously visible five years later, in 1884, when Arnold wrote the fifth and final of his 'Letters of an Old Playgoer.'

IV

THE first of these letters was the result of an invitation from Henry Arthur Jones to attend the first performance of the 'Silver King' on November 16, 1882; and the other four followed at irregular intervals during the next two years, called forth by one or another of the "current attractions" at the London theaters. It is plain enough

that he enjoyed writing them, pleased at the new
opportunity to apply the old doctrine and glad to
note the signs of the coming of a modern English
drama, slowly purging itself of fantasticality.
When Morley exprest his liking for these letters,
Arnold called them "the last flicker of a nearly
exhausted rushlight." Yet they still have illumination for us, more than thirty years later. They
deal with both of the aspects of the double art
of the drama, with the plays themselves and with
the performers who made them live at the moment. They disclose Arnold's constant sanity,
his penetrating shrewdness, his ability to see the
thing as it is, his cogency of presentation, his
power of drawing out the principle from the practice, and his insistence on finding the moral latent
in every manifestation of art.

In the performance of the 'Silver King' Arnold
noted "the high general level of the acting," and
he contrasted this with his memories of thirty-five
years earlier when Macready was acting his
great Shaksperian parts, supported by two or
three middling actors, "and the rest moping and
mowing in what was not to be called English but
rather stagese,"—a remark to be recommended
to the consideration of those praisers of past times
who still talk of the palmy days and who affect
to believe that the level of acting is lower than it
was when the old stock-companies strutted to half-
empty houses in dingy and shabby theaters.

He found that the 'Silver King' was an honest melodrama, relying "for its main effect on an outer drama of sensational incidents," that is to say, upon its external action, rather than on its characters. But melodrama as it was in its structure, the 'Silver King' was not melodramatic in its dialog. "In general thruout the piece the diction and the sentiments are natural; they have sobriety and propriety; they are literature."

In the second and third letters he dealt with three comedy-dramas, 'Forget-me-not' by Grove and Merivale, 'A Great Catch' by Hamilton Aidé, and 'Impulse' by Charles Stephenson. The plays of Aidé and of Grove and Merivale were evidences of the immediate development of a modern drama in England, far superior in veracity and in execution to the adaptations which had held the stage in London half-a-century earlier. Arnold credited 'Forget-me-not' with dialog "always pointed and smart, sometimes quite brilliant"; and he declared that "the piece has its life from its ability and verve." But with his usual insight he could not fail to see that its action lackt an adequate motive. In this respect 'A Great Catch' was more satisfactory; yet once again he was able to put his finger on the defect; one of the most important characters was inadequately developt. Here Arnold's criticism is purely technical; and it is sound and useful. Then he gave high praise to the admirable acting

281

of Genevieve Ward, an American who had taken a foremost position on the English stage.

'Impulse,' he did not like at all: "a piece more unprofitable it is hard to imagine." Stephenson's play was a flagrant example of the fantasticality, of the incurable falsity, likely to result from the dislocation of a plot essentially French in an absurd effort to adjust it to social conditions essentially English. The story no longer represents French life and it misrepresents English life; it becomes "something half-true, factitious and unmeaning." So the play is "intensely disagreeable," achieving success because of the acting of the two chief parts, because of "the singularly attractive, sympathetic and popular personalities of Mr. and Mrs. Kendal; while they are on the stage it is hard to be dissatisfied."

The three plays considered in the first two letters were evidences that dramatists were coming forward in England who were capable not only of invention and construction, but who were possest also of a sincere desire to deal with life as they severally saw it; and the single play considered in the third letter was evidence that the public had not yet experienced a change of heart and still lingered in the condition when it could be amused by insincere adaptations. In the fourth and fifth letters Arnold had worthier topics. The fourth letter was devoted to Henry Irving's sumptuous and brilliant presentation of 'Much

Ado About Nothing'; and the fifth and final letter, the only one written after his visit to America, after his voyage across "the unplumbed, salt, estranging sea," was devoted to Wilson Barrett's ambitious presentation of 'Hamlet.'

Arnold asserted that 'Much Ado' was beautifully put upon the stage, which "greatly heightens the charm of ideal comedy." He declared also that it was "acted with an evenness, a general level of merit which was not to be found twenty-five years ago." He discovered in Henry Irving and also in Ellen Terry "a personality which peculiarly fits them for ideal comedy. Miss Terry is sometimes restless and over-excited; but she has a spirited vivacity which is charming. Mr. Irving has faults which have often been pointed out; but he has, as an actor, a merit which redeems them all, and which is the secret of his success: the merit of delicacy and distinction. . . . Mankind are often unjust to this merit, and most of us much resist having to exhibit it in our own life and soul; but it is singular what a charm it exercises over us."

Arnold begins his criticism on Wilson Barrett's Hamlet with a discussion of the tragedy itself and with the influence exerted upon Shakspere himself at the very moment of its composition by Montaigne. This leads him to the rather strange conclusion that 'Hamlet' is "not a drama followed with perfect comprehension and profoundest emotion, which is the ideal for tragedy, but a problem, soliciting interpretation and solution. It will never, therefore, be a piece to be seen with pure satisfaction by those who will not deceive themselves. But such is its power and such is its fame that it will always continue to be acted, and we shall all of us continue to go to see it." Then the critic turns to the acting, praising E. S. Willard's Claudius and finding Wilson Barrett's Hamlet "fresh, natural, young, prepossessing, animated, coherent, the piece moves. All Hamlets I have seen dissatisfy us in something. Macready wanted person, Charles Kean mind, Fechter English; Mr. Wilson Barrett wants elocution."

V

As we read these 'Letters of An Old Playgoer' we cannot help noting three things; first, Arnold's alert interest in the drama as an art and his insight into its principles; second, his equally alert interest in acting and his understanding of its methods,—an understanding quite unusual among men of letters, who are generally even more at sea in discussing the histrionic art than they are in discussing the arts of the painter, the sculptor, and the architect. And it is significant that Arnold's own appreciation of dramaturgic and histrionic craftsmanship was not accompanied by any correspondingly acute appreciation of either pictorial

284

or plastic skill, in the manifestations of which he seems never to have been greatly interested, even during his visits to Italy and France.

The third thing we note is that Arnold retained his openmindedness and his freshness of impression. He was sixty when he turned aside to consider the improving conditions of the English theater, the advance in English acting and the beginnings of the modern English drama; but he revealed none of the customary sexagenarian proneness to look back longingly to the days of his youth, and to bewail the degeneracy discoverable in the years of his old age. He was quick to see progress and frank in acknowledging its presence. Perhaps his openmindedness in his maturity was in some measure due to his early and severe training in Greek and to his absorption of the free Greek spirit, which secured him against pedantry and kept his vision unimpaired.

(1916.)

XVI

MEMORIES OF EDWIN BOOTH

I

MY earliest recollection of Edwin Booth goes back to 1865, when I was taken to the Winter Garden Theater to see one of the hundred consecutive performances of 'Hamlet'—the longest run that any play of Shakspere's had ever had (up to that time) in any city in the world. I find that all I can recall of the play, then seen for the first time, is a misty memory of the moonlit battlements of Elsinore with the gray figure of the Ghost as he solemnly stalkt forward. A few weeks later in that same winter I was allowed to see Booth again, as Richelieu; and I can more readily recapture the thrill with which I heard him threaten to launch the curse of Rome. I have an impression that the scenery for 'Richelieu' had been painted in Paris; and I think that even now after the lapse of more than half-a-century I can visualize the spacious and beautiful hall in which Richelieu had his interview with Marion Delorme.

In 1869, when I was scant seventeen, I had the good fortune to be present at the opening of

Booth's own theater, the handsomest playhouse which had ever been erected in New York and the most elaborately equipt. The play was 'Romeo and Juliet'; and the part of the impulsive heroine was taken by Mary McVickar, whom Booth was soon to marry. The only picture still imprinted on my memory is the lovely garden, flooded with moonlight, as Juliet appeared on the balcony and as Romeo lightly overleapt the walls.

After I attained to man's estate I saw Booth in all his great parts—excepting only Richard II, which he did not long retain in his repertory. The sinister malignity of his Pescara (in Shiel's 'Apostate') has etcht itself in my memory; and so also has the demoniac dance of Bertuccio (in the 'Fool's Revenge') when the deeply outraged jester believes that he has been able at last to repay in full the injury he had received from his enemy. As the audience knows that it is not his enemy's wife but his own beloved daughter that he has just helpt to abduct, the tragic irony of the poignant situation was intensified by the few irrepressible capers of the hunchback, an effect as daring as it was successful, and possible only to an actor of imagination and of unfailing certainty of execution.

Altho I saw Edwin Booth often on the stage I did not have the pleasure of making his acquaintance until about 1884, three or four years before he founded The Players,—which opened its doors just before midnight on the last day of 1888. One of my good friends, Laurence Hutton was a good friend of Booth's; and when Hutton and I, Lawrence Barrett, Frank Millet and E. A. Abbey organized a little dinner club, called The Kinsmen, Booth was one of the first of the practitioners of the several allied arts whom we askt to join us. In private life he was unaffected and unassuming, gentle, simple, modest,—altho he was naturally dignified and altho he could not but be conscious of his position at the head of the American stage.

It has been my privilege to know fairly well the leaders of the dramatic profession, in the later years of the nineteenth century, Booth and Irving, Jefferson and Coquelin, Salvini and Barnay; they were none of them openly vainglorious or even unduly self-centered; and perhaps Booth was the least pretentious of them all. He had the saving sense of humor; and while he took his work seriously he did not take himself too seriously. In fact, when I read his familiar correspondence, lovingly set in order by his devoted daughter, I recognized the man disclosed in these letters as the very man whose characteristics Sargent captured and fixt forever in the illuminating portrait which E. C. Benedict presented to The Players. There was a certain transparency about his character; and in private life his personality was very winning—a quality which on the

288

stage transmuted itself into what is often termed "magnetism."

II

AT the supper which The Kinsmen gave when we welcomed Irving as a member,—it had to be a supper and not a dinner since Irving was acting every night—chance placed me at table between Booth and Irving. I noted with appreciation the high friendliness of their association, devoid of any suspicion of jealousy or even of rivalry, altho one of them was the acknowledged leader of the American stage and the other was the undisputed chief of the British theater. It was evident that their cordiality was not put on for the occasion only and that they really liked one another and were glad to foregather for the interchange of experiences. Of course, their talk soon turned to their profession and to the mighty actors who had preceded them. I soon discovered that Irving had never been greatly interested in the performers of an earlier generation; he was familiar enough with the careers of Macready and of Charles Kean, who were his immediate predecessors, but he had not cared to study the lives of Edmund Kean, of George Frederick Cooke and of the Kembles, who had been the leaders of the stage two generations earlier. Of course, it is never necessary for an artist to be a student of the biographical history of his art; for him it is sufficient if he has spent his strength on mastering its principles and in training himself to apply them.

Booth's devotion to the memory of his father, the Junius Brutus Booth who had been hailed as a rival of Edmund Kean, had lured him into the study of the lives of all of his father's more important contemporaries. While he could not be called a bookish man, he owned most of the volumes of histrionic criticism and of theatrical biography which elucidate the history of the English-speaking stage in the first half of the nineteenth century. Not only did he own them, he had read them; and by their aid his father's fellow-players had become living men to him. He had accumulated anecdotes about them and he had studied out their methods. As he had found this reading instructive as well as interesting he assumed that Irving had done the same; and in reviving these half-forgotten figures, already going into the night, one and all, Booth frankly took for granted Irving's equal intimacy with them. Apparently Irving saw no reason to undeceive him, and without in any way pretending to an exhaustive acquaintance with careers of his renowned predecessors, he was able to throw in from time to time an apt anecdote,—which had probably come to him by oral tradition.

Booth was three years older than Irving; in 1861 when he was not yet thirty and already a star of proclaimed promise, he paid his first professional visit to England; and in Manchester, Irving, then only an obscure stock actor, supported him. A score of years later when Irving was the prosperous manager of the foremost theater in England, Booth again ventured across the Atlantic to act in London. His season was none too successful financially, partly because he had unwisely allowed himself to be taken to the wrong theater. With characteristic kindliness Irving invited Booth to join him for a month at the Lyceum to alternate the characters of Othello and Iago and to have the aid of Ellen Terry as Desdemona. This was in the spring of 1881; and for four weeks the Lyceum was crowded to its full capacity.

A friend of mine, who had played one of the parts in the tragedy, described the rehearsals to me and dwelt on the unfailing courtesy with which Irving, as the host, sought always to make Booth, as the guest, feel at home. Whenever they came to a scene in which Booth appeared, Irving would ask how he would prefer to have the action arranged; and with equal courtesy Booth would leave the settling of the business to Irving, suggesting only when it was necessary. "This is the way I usually do it." My friend noticed that Irving seemed surprized, and perhaps even a little shockt, that Booth set so little store by the details of stage-management. And here the most markt difference between these two great actors stood revealed.

Booth was an actor, first of all, and he was a stage-manager only in so far as stage management might be necessary for the effect which he himself desired to make as an actor. Perhaps it would not be fair to say that Irving was primarily a stage-manager; but it is not unfair to suggest that he was a stage-manager of extraordinary fertility of invention and that he was accustomed to use his skill as a stage-manager to support his efforts as an actor. Booth was always careful about his own effects, his own business; but he relied mainly on himself and upon his own individual power as an actor. So it was that he was less interested in the play as a whole and in those scenes in which he did not himself appear. Irving, on the other hand, was insistent in getting the smallest details exactly to his taste, holding with Michael Angelo that "trifles make perfection, and perfection is no trifle." Perhaps this difference in their attitude explains why it was that Booth was unsuccessful in the management of the theater he had built for himself and that Irving managed his theater triumphantly for more than a score of years.

It is possible that Irving never himself perceived how truly magnanimous he had been in inviting Booth to appear with him at the Lyceum. In the first week when Booth was Othello and

Irving Iago there was a comparative equality between them. Booth had the amplitude of elocution and the fiery passion which Othello demanded; and Irving was a brilliant and picturesque Iago. But the second week, when they exchanged parts, the comparative equality disappeared. Fine as Booth was as Othello he was even finer as Iago, whom he represented as the incarnation of implacable malignity, whereas Irving lackt the simple utterance and the massive emotion required for the adequate performance of Othello. It would be going too far to suggest that Irving failed as Othello; he was too clever, too experienced and too richly endowed to fail in anything he undertook. Yet it may be said not unfairly that his Othello was among the least successful of his Shaksperian characters, ranking with his spasmodic Romeo and far below his graceful and noble Hamlet.

III

It was after Irving's first visit to the United States that he took part in a discussion with Coquelin as to the completeness with which the actor ought actually to feel the emotion he is expressing. Coquelin had declared that Diderot's 'Paradox on Acting'—to the effect that the performer must have felt the emotion while he is studying the part but that he must not feel it

too acutely on the stage or it will interfere with
his certainty of execution—Coquelin had declared
that this was not a paradox, but only a plain
statement of the indisputable fact. Irving had
denied this, asserting that the actor needs to be
moved by the actual passion when he is expressing it. I recall that Joseph Jefferson told me
that he thought they were both right, each from
his own point of view, and each advocating the
method he himself had found satisfactory—Coquelin merely recalling the emotion he had originally felt and Irving allowing himself to feel it
again and again as amply as he could.

When I spoke to Booth about Diderot's 'Paradox,' he said that he thought that there was more
in it than Irving was willing to admit; and he
illustrated this opinion by an experience of his
own. One night when he was acting in the
'Fool's Revenge,' he saw his daughter sitting in a
stage-box; and this reminded him that he, like
Bertuccio, had an only daughter whom he loved
devotedly. This thought kept recurring as the
play advanced; and he was conscious that his
own paternal affection was making him identify
himself more than ever before with the hunchback father whom he was portraying. He found
that he was putting himself into the place of Bertuccio and asking how he would feel if his own
daughter, then before his eyes, had the sorrowful
fate of the heroine of the play. It had seemed

to him that, as a result of this intensified personal emotion, he had never acted the character with so much poignancy of pathos. Yet when his daughter took him home in a carriage, she askt what had been the matter with him that evening, since she had never seen him impersonate Bertuccio so ineffectively. Here was a case where excess of actual feeling had interfered with the self-control needed for the complete artistic expression of the emotion.

Irving may have exprest his opinion with more emphasis than was warranted; and Coquelin was quite as intolerant in maintaining his. I must confess that I thought Coquelin a little extreme in his insistence on the necessity of absolute freedom from emotion when the actor was before the audience. In one of our many talks about the art of acting, he once went so far as to assert that after he had seen a certain actress shed real tears at a moment of emotional tension, this accomplisht performer immediately sank in his estimation, since her weeping seemed to him to reveal an absence of the complete self-control which a fine artist ought always to possess.

Booth's famous father, so his son has recorded, endeavored always to sink his own personality in that of the character he was performing. "Whatever the part he had to impersonate, he was, from the time of its rehearsal until he slept at night, imbued with its very essence. If

'Othello' was billed for the evening, he would, perhaps, wear a crescent pin on his breast that day.
. . . If Shylock was to be his part at night, he was a Jew all day; and, if in Baltimore at the time, he would pass hours with a learned Israelite, discussing Hebrew history." During the actual performance of one of these mighty characters with which he had thus sought to identify himself, he was possest by the passion which surged from the progressive situations of the play. "At the instant of intense emotion, when the spectators were enthralled by his magnetic influence . . . he would whisper some silliness or make a face" while his head was turned from the audience. His fellow-actors attributed his conduct at such times to lack of feeling, whereas it was in reality, so Edwin Booth testified, due to his "extreme excess of feeling."

IV

In 1884 Laurence Hutton and I made preparations to edit a book about the theater upon a novel plan; and a year or two later we sent forth at intervals the five volumes entitled 'Actors and Actresses of Great Britain and the United States, from the days of David Garrick to the present time.' We carefully selected about eighty performers of acknowledged prominence, each in his own generation; and we wrote ourselves or had written by experts in histrionic history, brief but carefully documented biographies, appending to the sketch of every performer's career excerpts from contemporary dramatic criticism, from memoirs and reminiscences, and from collections of theatrical anecdotes, so as to depict from several angles the men and women who were sitting for their portraits. Our friends came generously to our assistance, more especially those devoted students of stage-history, William Winter and William Archer. Austin Dobson enrich our first volume with a delightful account of the varied activities of David Garrick; and H. C. Bunner contributed to our fifth volume an equally delightful account of Joseph Jefferson.

The article on Edwin Booth was prepared by Lawrence Barrett; and Edwin Booth himself was to prepare that on his father. Irving willingly agreed to write the paper on Edmund Kean; but when the time came he askt us to release him from his promise. So we turned to Edwin Booth again and requested him to give us the sketch of Kean to accompany that which he had already written on Kean's sometime rival, Junius Brutus Booth; and he allowed himself to be persuaded. I think that the writing of these two papers was Edwin Booth's first venture into literature, since his valuable notes on the acting of Othello and of Shylock were prepared a little later. To write was for him a novel experience, and he was modestly diffident, postponing the unwonted task until at last the spirit moved him; then he sat himself down to the work and poured forth his unpremeditated recollections of his father with the precipitancy with which he might write a letter.

Even after he had set down what was in his heart he hesitated to let the manuscript pass out of his own hands. When Hutton was at last empowered to carry it off, he brought it to me; and it made glad our editorial souls. It was not at all in accord with the pattern accepted by the professional writers who had prepared the articles for the earlier volumes. It did not give the facts of its subject's career in strict chronological sequence, with the obligatory dates in their proper places. It contained no dates and only a few facts; but it did give what was better than all the panoply of information,—an illuminating interpretation of an extraordinary character by the one person who knew him best and loved him most.

It was thrown on paper in haste; it had not been modified by second thoughts; its sentences were sometimes entangled; and its punctuation was eccentric. But these external inadvertences were negligible. To precede Booth's tribute to his father and to be distinguisht from it by a difference of type, we prepared an outline biography of Junius Brutus with all the missing facts and all the obligatory dates; and we then had Booth's own manuscript copied faithfully, whereupon we made the few adjustments necessary to bring it into conformity with the conventions of literature. The result stood forth as an admirable piece of writing, individual in expression, full of flavor, and rich in sympathetic understanding. It may be noted that actors, when they can write at all, generally write well, perhaps because their profession has trained them to avoid prolixity while its practice has stored their memory with a vocabulary as varied as it is vigorous.

Encouraged by our editorial appreciation, Edwin Booth wrote out for us his impressions of Kean, inspired in some measure by the study of Kean's death-mask. He told us that altho Edmund Kean and Junius Brutus Booth had been rivals in London, there was no personal enmity in their contest for the crown, and when they came together again in America their meeting was not only friendly but cordial. That the two great actors were not hostile to each other was made certain by this glowing tribute to Edmund Kean written by the son of Junius Brutus Booth, as it had been made probable years before by the appearance of Junius Brutus Booth as the Second Actor in support of the Hamlet of Edmund Kean's son.

Doubtful as Edwin Booth had been as to his ability to put on paper adequately his impressions of Kean and Booth, he was keenly interested in their reception by his friends after they were printed in the third volume of our 'Actors and Actresses.' In the correspondence lovingly collected by his daughter he is constantly mentioning his "little sketches," anxious to learn what his friends thought of them. As an actor he was surfeited with newspaper criticism and he had come to pay little attention to it; but as a writer he wanted to see every journalistic review of our volume which might comment on his two contributions. It is amusing; in fact, it is almost pathetic, to note the new interest which the writing of these two articles had brought into his life when he was beginning to be wearied, and to observe the eagerness with which he awaited any casual comment on what he had written. I am glad to be able to record that the two brief essays were highly valued by those most competent to appreciate them.

V

ONE of the most intelligent and accomplisht actors of the present day has made it a rule not to read the incessant newspaper notices of his performance; and he once gave me an excellent reason for his decision:—"If the criticism is unfriendly, it is likely to disturb me at my work,—and if it is friendly it is likely to increase my natural conceit!" I think that this would have won the approval of Edwin Booth. I recall that when I once askt him if he had ever been benefited by any of the criticisms of his acting, he responded at once "Never!" Then, after a moment's pause and with his good-humored smile he added, "That's not quite true. Sometimes, in one of the little cities, the theatrical critic points out that I have been careless in the performance of this scene or that; and sometimes I have seen that he was right. But that is the only benefit I ever got from anything of the sort."

He held that it was not good for the actor to associate with those whose duty it was to criticize his artistic endeavors. For this reason he suggested that critics of acting should not be admitted to The Players; and to this day and after thirty years that is the unwritten law of the club he founded. He regretted greatly that this ruling excluded his cherisht friend, William Winter; but he did not wish us to make a single exception. I believe that it was in his thought that it would be unfortunate if the actor should be tempted to make up to the critics and to get on the blind side of them, so to speak. Perhaps he had also in mind two other reasons for his request. The first is that artists of all kinds, and perhaps the actors more especially, are prone to express exaggerated opinions of one another's work, opinions extravagantly favorable and sometimes extravagantly unfavorable;—opinions which it would be undesirable to have overheard by outsiders. And the second is that as the actor's canvas on which he paints his picture and the actor's clay with which he models his statue, are his own person, his own features, his own members, any criticism of his achievement, or of his failure to achieve, is necessarily personal,—possibly so personal as to make it unpleasant for artist and critic to have to sit at meat together.

It was after he made his home at The Players— where the room in which he lived and died is piously kept exactly as he left it—that I had more frequent opportunities of meeting him. He liked to come down to the reading-room and the dining-room and to mingle freely with his fellow-members, and to have them accept him as one of themselves and not set him apart as the Founder of the club. As it chanced he used to spend at least a portion of the later summers of his life with his daughter at Narragansett Pier, almost exactly opposite my own summer home. Sometimes he came over to see us and sometimes we went over to call on him.

I regret now that I did not make notes of the more interesting things he said in one or another of our talks. I can recapture only a few of them. He told me that the conditions of the theater were very primitive when he first began to act in support of his father; and in 'Richard III,' for instance, when the time came for Richard to fight Richmond, his father used to go to the wings on one side of the stage as the actor of Richmond went to the wings on the other side; and each of them seized by the hilt a combat-sword thrust out by an invisible stage-hand, whereupon they went back to the center of the stage and began their fight to the death. He also confest that he had been inclined to doubt the wisdom of his having discarded Colley Cibber's perversion of 'Richard III'—a fiery and bombastic adaptation which had held the stage for two centuries and which was really more effective theatrically than the reverent rearrangement of Shakspere's own text which Booth had substituted for it.

I happened once to mention Irving's taking Ellen Terry and his whole company to West Point to play the 'Merchant of Venice' in the Mess Hall on a platform draped only with American flags and therefore without any scenery; and I remarkt that Irving had assured me that the power of the play was in no wise lessened by the enforced deprivation of all decorative aid. To cap this Booth told me about his unexpected misadventure at Waterbury. He arrived at the theater to be informed that the costumes had not been delivered. Scenery and properties had come all right, but the trunks containing the dresses for 'Hamlet' could not be found. Booth inquired about the advance sale of tickets and learnt that every seat had been sold. "Very well, then," he said, "we must not disappoint an audience. We'll give the play in the clothes we have on!" When the time came he sent the manager before the curtain to explain the situation and to announce that any spectator who was not satisfied with the prospect could have his money back from the box-office.

"Of course, nobody left the house," he commented smiling. "But you should have seen the fright of the company—especially the women—at the idea of appearing in a Shaksperian tragedy in the dresses they wore to travel in. They got over that, as soon as they found that the effect of strangeness quickly wore off. After the first act, Robert Pateman, who did not appear as the Gravedigger until the fifth act, and who had gone in front to judge the effect, came round behind to reassure his wife, who was our Ophelia. He explained that there were little runs of laughter every now and then during the opening scenes but that these soon died down, until toward the end of the act the performance was apparently as effective as if we had all been garbed with historic propriety. It was an odd experience, —and perhaps the most amusing part of it was that the trunks containing the costumes were discovered at last in a heap outside the railroad station!"

On another occasion he told me about a little discussion he had had with Jefferson when 'Rip Van Winkle' was first produced at Booth's Theater. He had wanted his old friend to be pleased and he had prepared entirely new scenery. The set for the first act, the home from which Rip is to be driven out by his shrewish wife, was a careful reconstitution of a characteristic kitchen in a Catskill farmhouse, with a kettle swinging on a crane before a glowing fire. But at the dress rehearsal when Jefferson made his entrance, he stopt short and called out sharply "Take that thing away!"—that thing was the gas-log blazing brightly; "I don't want people to be looking at that. I want them to look at me!" The rehearsal waited while the objectionable distraction was removed. When the first act had been gone thru, Booth called Jefferson's attention to the black gap where the log had been and he askt if that might not draw the eyes of the spectators away from Rip's features. "Perhaps you are right," Jefferson admitted; "have the log put back—but don't light it. I don't want it to sparkle and hiss."

Fifty years ago a gas-log was a novelty and it might have diverted the gaze and thereby interfered momentarily with the current of dramatic sympathy. Of course, it was not personal vanity, but a due respect for art, which led Jefferson to declare that he wanted people to look at him all the time. When he played Rip the true center of interest was Rip's ever-changing countenance.

Unless my memory plays me false it was in this same conversation with Booth that he told me of a remark Charlotte Cushman had made to him when they were rehearsing 'Macbeth.' "You must not be afraid of overdoing the part," she had said. "Remember that Macbeth is the father of all the stage-villains!"

(1919.)